Corporate Venturing: A Survival Guide

CORPORATE VENTURING:

A SURVIVAL GUIDE

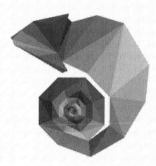

*It's not the biggest or fastest that survives
but the most adaptable to change*

HEIDI MASON

ELIZABETH ARRINGTON

JAMES MAWSON

Corporate Venturing: A Survival Guide
It's not the biggest or fastest that survives, but the most adaptable to change.

Published 2019

ISBN-13: 9781999369903

Published by:
• Global Corporate Venturing (London, England)

Paperback and e-book editions produced via Kindle Direct Publishing Platform, Amazon

The authors wish to express their gratitude and appreciation for the invaluable contributions and ongoing assistance of the CV professionals and partners who so willingly invested their own time and effort in support of this book's development. We'd like to especially acknowledge the eight CV program teams and their corporate compatriots who collaborated with us to produce profiles of their high-performance programs. So, to the teams at Capital One Growth Ventures, Citi Ventures, CSAA SI, Echo Health Ventures, Intel Capital, JetBlue Technology Ventures, Merck Global Health Innovation, and Munich Re Ventures: Thank you for sharing your journeys. Thanks also to industry leaders Wendell Brooks and Sue Siegel for their insights, offered in the Foreword and Afterword.

And, finally, a special thank you to our families and friends for their patience and support throughout our development of this book.

Table of Contents

Preface

Corporate venturing has never mattered more. This is a time when the world's and your parent company's interest in corporate venturing is at its peak. Corporate venturing has earned a position of respect among portfolio companies and partners for the multipliers of value it delivers, and corporate venturing leaders have a "seat at the table" in setting corporate strategy, joining the handful of the highest-level executives who determine the company's present and future course.

But this is what hasn't changed: corporate venturing is *incredibly* hard to do well, and in a way that lasts.

Even when high-performing teams closely follow the best practices derived from other programs' models and professionals' experiences and impeccably execute everything required for program and team development, they are often impeded—even stopped dead in their tracks—by unpredictable events and decisions totally independent of their programs and outside of their control.

This is the "baseline," the wholly natural reality for CV programs and their parent companies, around which corporate venturing teams must "duck and weave" if their programs are to survive—and not just in the start-up phase, but continuously, throughout cycles for CV program expansion and scale.

And it is for this reason that we wanted to write this book. The authors have spent decades immersed in the business of corporate venturing, now in its watershed "Fifth Wave" of practice and program evolution. We united to write *Corporate Venturing: A Survival Guide*, armed with our complementary business histories, a decade of previous collaborations and an aspiration: to translate the complexities of corporate venturing into a simpler, more accessible narrative and "common language" for participants:

- For framing the context, investment levels, value creation and critical positioning of corporate venturing in today's broader innovation investment ecosystem
- For breaking down "agile" CV program and practice development into its most critical actions and accomplishments, at three pivotal points in its growth

Finally, there is no greater way to learn than by example. Selected high-performer corporate venturing programs have generously shared the stories of their own development in this book—the who, what, and why of

- how they were formed;
- how they have accelerated and adapted their portfolio strategies and managed their internal and external partnerships;
- how they deliver on expectations for their performance.

So, corporate venturing professionals, this book is for you, intended as a "shorthand" guide for you and your management as you craft and scale meaningful corporate venturing programs. We also hope it will provide insight, and perhaps greater appreciation, for what you do and all the moving parts you manage on behalf of the venture teams you champion, as well as the many investment and business partners with whom you connect.

Foreword

A fundamental rule in technology says that whatever can
be done will be done. You need to try to do the impossible.
—ANDY GROVE, FORMER CHAIRMAN AND
CEO OF INTEL CORPORATION

Since 2016, I have had the privilege of running Intel Capital, one of the longest-running corporate venture organizations in the tech industry. Through up and down economic cycles, strategic pivots, and technology shifts, Intel Capital has consistently invested and driven value for our parent company, Intel. We do this by having a relentless focus on delivering value to our portfolio companies. I believe that we've played a role in trying to do the impossible. We're the forward looking, visionary arm of Intel. We are at the epicenter of an amazing community of entrepreneurs driving new technologies forward—from AI, autonomous and flying cars, and advances in data analytics, to smart cities, smart factories, and beyond.

One of the reasons I am passionate about my job as president of Intel Capital is that I can leverage the resources of Intel, the world's greatest engineering company. I believe there is a triangle of growth and innovation for large corporations with three elements: organic efforts, equity investing, and M&A.

- At the top of the triangle sits research and development. Typically, this is where large companies invest the most. One-hundred-percent-owned products developed through R&D also have the highest return. At Intel we have a long history of technology and process innovation, and we have many smart people working in our organization. But we don't have the market cornered on smart engineers, so we also…

- Make investments in outsider disruptors and entrepreneurs through Intel Capital. This second point on the triangle allows us to place meaningful bets on unproven technologies being developed outside of Intel. We look for driven people that are trying to tackle big problems—driving change in the entire ecosystem. We also look for places that Intel can add value to the start-up.
- The final point on the triangle is M&A—both transformational and tech and talent acquisitions. We use M&A to fill the holes where R&D and Intel Capital have missed. Transformational M&A can expand an addressable market or create a new business. Smaller tech and talent M&A opportunities allow us to complement a BU strategy, fill a product gap, or accelerate our roadmap and route to market.

Having these three elements as a solid base to examine both innovation and disruption allows companies such as Intel to evolve and thrive.

Equity investing can be an efficient use of capital when looking for innovation and growth. Although CVCs vary in how they balance strategic versus financial investing, most fall into a continuum of being financially focused and strategically relevant. If our returns as CVCs exceed the weighted average cost of capital for our parent companies, we have effectively "made money" and also gained valuable intelligence about the larger ecosystem. Internally, I call this "getting paid to learn."

Corporate venture capital organizations not only play a role in the growth of our parent companies, but also bring the resources of our organizations to help our portfolio companies succeed. These resources include technology endorsement, customer introductions, access to engineering/technical expertise, business unit collaboration, and company talent building. At Intel Capital, if we can't add value for our portfolio company beyond dollars, we don't invest.

I am a strong advocate for partnering in the CVC industry. When we work together to share deal flow and add value to our portfolio companies, we can completely differentiate performance. I believe there is a multiplier effect when several CVCs bring our unique set of resources to the table. At Intel Capital we are committed to building a syndicate of CVCs that want to drive success for technology investing.

Recently, venture capital has outperformed many other asset classes, causing many corporate CEOs and boards to take notice. This book can help you understand the corporate venture landscape and how CVCs can produce sustainable results for their stakeholders.

- If you are looking to create a CVC practice, this book outlines approaches and considerations to review as you formulate your program.
- If you are a leader or member of a CVC today, you will find ideas on how to articulate the value of your organization to your CEO, your board, and your peers. You can benchmark against CVCs at each phase of maturity and assess your own CVC journey.
- If you are contemplating a career in corporate venturing, this book provides insights into the many different ways CVCs are structured, operated, and measured.
- If you are a financial VC, you may find ideas on how to partner with CVCs to drive value beyond dollars invested.
- Finally, if you are an entrepreneur considering working with a CVC, you will gain understanding into the breadth of resources CVCs can bring to the table, and you will learn how to assess the mission and mandate of your potential funding partner.

My team will tell you that there is nothing I enjoy more than forming a hypothesis and having a debate. This is one of the key things that makes my job as a venture investor exciting. My hypothesis around corporate venture capital is simple: CVCs can deliver value to our portfolio companies beyond our financial investments, and we are effectively paid to learn.

I hope that as you read this book you will consider this hypothesis, and I welcome you to reach out to me and my team or to Global Corporate Venturing or the authors if you'd like to engage in the debate.

Wendell Brooks
President, Intel Capital

CHAPTER 1

Introduction: Global Corporate Venturing Industry's Past, Present, and Future

Executive Summary

Once upon a time, venture capital was a niche industry helping entrepreneurs grow by providing capital and advice, and corporations mainly tried to be like VCs.

Every day, corporations would look at deals brought to them by VCs and would ask to pay a premium to join the round or buy the portfolio company.

One day, after the global financial crisis, and as the implications of Henry Chesbrough's open innovation theory, published in 2003, became better understood, corporations decided venturing was more strategic to their future.

Because of that they set up CVCs as part of their innovation toolset and invested more time, support, and money to find deals, lead them, and help portfolio companies impact their parents.

Consequently, the venture industry and corporations started to change. The industry became larger and global and part of a merging of private and public capital markets. It became more strategic, while beginning to show financial gains, and corporations started to change as CVC influenced mergers and acquisitions (M&A) and R&D and developed its own professional requirements.

Finally, venture was recognized as a service-orientated profession helping entrepreneurs with their five primary needs of capital, customers, product development, hiring, and an exit, and corporations opened up their value creation and shareholder returns options.

Introduction: Why This / Why Now?

Fred Wilson—a man known for his strong opinions—is at his most rabid on the topic of corporate VCs. Just more than five years ago, he said: "I am never, ever, ever, ever, ever going to do that again," adding in the video recording by PandoDaily in mid-2013 one more "ever!" just in case we didn't quite get it. Editor Sarah Lacey wrote of Wilson's comments that having a corporate investor in a venture syndicate has "repeatedly gone so badly in the past that it might be the one thing that makes him leave a board in the future."

Wilson is someone to listen to. His venture capital (VC) returns have been fantastic. The 2004-vintage fund posted a 67 percent annual performance result (called internal rate of return in the jargon), according to Oregon Public Employees Retirement Fund back in 2016.

And Wilson's venture capital firm, Union Square Ventures, has almost single-handedly developed New York City's innovation capital ecosystem into a globally relevant center with the second-highest concentration of tech talent after Silicon Valley in California, according to insights by start-up service AngelList in 2018, when online retailer Amazon chose the city as a site for an office.

Wilson, however, has been largely ignored by the two groups that he was trying to influence: the entrepreneurs selecting investors and the corporations funding them.

Corporate Venturing's Growth

Over the past five years, entrepreneurs have increasingly lapped up the corporate venture capitalists' money, and greater numbers of companies have thrown not just ever-larger amounts of it at them but also offered up a buffet of extra support to help the start-ups grow.

Over 1,000 active corporates per year

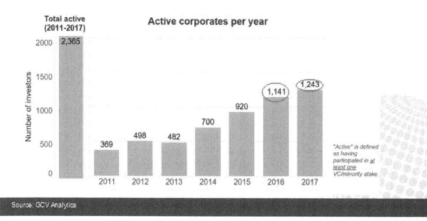

Money poured into the CVC arena and VC realm has been growing at the same pace

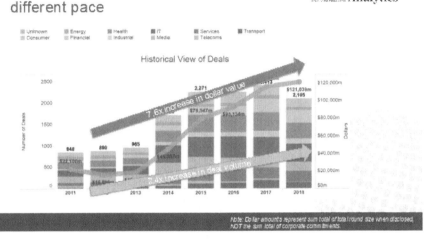

(Note: 2018 data through to end of October)

Collaboration the Goal

In interviews now, corporations and entrepreneurs talk about the disintermediation of VCs rather than whether they can find ways to work together.

Ferran Prat, senior vice president of research administration and industry relations at the MD Anderson Cancer Center in Houston, Texas, onstage at Global Corporate Venturing's (GCV) Venture Houston conference in November 2018 said: "There is a shrinking role for VCs. Industry is bringing ideas in-house and taking more risk. At MD Anderson we are trying to bring ideas to the point that pharma can bring them internally. The window for VCs is narrowing."

Wendell Brooks, president of Intel Capital, talks about CVCs investing alongside one another as "we are better together."

Start-ups have long understood the power of diversity among their investors. Why have just one corporate venture in a round if you can have several?

E-Volo has Intel and car maker Daimler in its syndicate, and Florian Reuter, CEO of the company (better known as Volocopter), said at Intel Capital's 2018 Global Summit that the flying-car maker's founders had tried to effectively create a whole new category of travel by coming to the industry as software engineers rather than domain experts.

Within three years, if regulatory approval granted as expected, then "mobility as a service" could make it easy to fly from an airport into the center of a city in 30 minutes for the cost of a taxi but in less time, Reuter said. Volocopter is among several start-up initiatives being tried, including another Intel Capital portfolio company, Joby, as well as Tencent-backed Lilium, JetBlue-backed Zunum and Uber's Elevate project.

In his 2011 manifesto "What Happened to the Future," investor Peter Thiel drily noted: "We wanted flying cars, instead we got 140 characters [Twitter's messaging limitation at the time]."

Inside a decade, Thiel might have his wish but through collaboration between start-ups and large corporations.

And it is worth looking more closely at the collaboration between corporations inside syndicates as much as between them and start-ups. As the leaders of the GCV Powerlist 100 show, the next step in the industry is now coming as much from the leaders thinking about their syndicates with each other as with whether or how to convince management to invest in start-ups and how to do so, as this battle has effectively already been won over the past five or so years.

Venture has traditionally relied on personal connections or meeting at the door of the portfolio company through chance to form syndicates. Institutionalizing the process and connections between CVCs fits corporations' often-international mandates and process-driven strengths.

But this cooperation has not always been the case, and Wilson's comments remain a valid warning.

Venture's History

Once upon a time, venture capital was a niche industry helping entrepreneurs grow by providing capital and advice.

Venture capital can be traced back to the earliest days of America's business giants. Bessemer Venture Partners (BVP) is the oldest venture capital firm in the United States, founded in 1911 as a family trust for Henry Phipps, a cofounder of Carnegie Steel, and only moving beyond the family in the 1970s.

And as data provider CB Insights notes in its history of CVC, it was 1914 when Pierre Samuel du Pont, acting president of chemical and plastics manufacturer DuPont, invested in a still-private, six-year-old automobile start-up named General Motors (GM).

After the war, the companies would become even more intertwined, CB Insights added. DuPont's board of directors invested $25 million in GM, betting the cash injection could speed GM's development, which in turn would also expand the demand for DuPont's own goods—including artificial leather, plastics, and paints—as well as serve as a promising investment. The company, which had gone public in 1916, was growing sales 56 percent annually, already had over eighty-five thousand employees, and had begun building a new Detroit headquarters for its executives.

DuPont would go on to help pioneer corporate venture capital.

First Wave of Corporate Venture Capital

This first flowering of venture stretched from the late 1950s and early'60s, the era of the Nifty 50 growth stocks with high valuations, until the stagflation crises of the 1970s.

In his history of venture capital, which was then primarily a US industry, Jerry Neumann writes, "The pioneers of the 1960s and 1970s had figured out a winning formula: build a great network to source opportunities, spend months getting to know the management team and doing due diligence, invest at the earliest possible stage, work hard to help founders get the right team in place and put together partnerships, and take the company public only when it was ready to be a public company."

Taking a leaf out of the funding models used in the Age of Exploration from Europe to the rest of the world in the fifteenth and sixteenth centuries, VCs charged the same taxes on entrepreneurs as sovereigns had done with their sailors. By law, all New World silver was delivered to a crown mint back in Spain and Portugal, and the royal treasury took its quinto (20 percent tax). Similarly, VCs and private equity executives, who have long styled themselves as kings of capital, charged a 20 percent performance fee (carried interest in the jargon) on successful deals on top of management fees.

The CVC model is less explicit. They rarely charge carried interest—the J Thelander Consulting 2018 survey of CVC compensation found a fifth (sixteen) of eighty-one corporate venturing respondents benefited from carry ranging from 2 to 18.5 percent, with the majority being rewarded with bonuses.

Gary Dushnitsky, associate professor of strategy and entrepreneurship at the London Business School, noted in the Coller Institute of Venture's 2015 history issue, that

> Historically, corporate venture capital exhibits highly cyclical patterns, both in terms of total investment amounts as well as in terms of the number of firms that engage in CVC. The mid-1960s saw the First Wave of corporate venture capital as a confluence of two distinct factors. It was stimulated by the success of pioneering independent venture capital funds and the stellar performance of their portfolio companies.
>
> The practice then diffused to established firms as part of the overall trend of corporate diversification in the 1960s, which was driven by excess cash flow accrued by many large US corporations. Approximately 25% of the Fortune 500 firms set up CVC programs during this period, including such firms as American Standard, Boeing, Dow, Exxon, Heinz, and WR Grace. Many programs invested in external as well as internal ventures (for example Exxon Enterprises funded 37 technology ventures where half were external to Exxon and the remainder internally grown).
>
> The oil shock and related macroeconomic changes left many CVC investing firms with little excess cash flows, thus choking investment activities. The collapse of the market for IPO in 1973, and an increasing number of frictions within the CVC programs and between the programs and their parent corporations, further contributed to the termination of almost all the programs.

Second Wave of CVC

Neumann notes the surviving VCs hunkered down before a late-1970s change in regulations allowed pension funds to consider it a "prudent" investment. The $2.5 billion managed by venture capital firms in 1977 quintupled by 1983 to $12 billion, according to *Venture Capital Journal* in July 1984, as cited by Neumann.

This again sparked a CVC resurgence. Dushnitsky said:

A Second Wave of corporate venture capital followed in the early 1980s.

A significant growth in technology-driven commercial opportunities, along with favorable public markets and legislative flexibility via the Employee Retirement Income Security Act in 1979, energized the venture capital market.

Again, many leading pharmaceutical companies (e.g., Johnson & Johnson), as well as the chemical and metal industries, launched corporate venture capital programs. Technology firms (e.g., Analog Devices, Control Data Systems, and Hewlett-Packard) also initiated new venture financing efforts. The 1987 market crash led to a sharp decline in independent, as well as corporate, venture capital activity.

Number of Funds, by Vintage Year

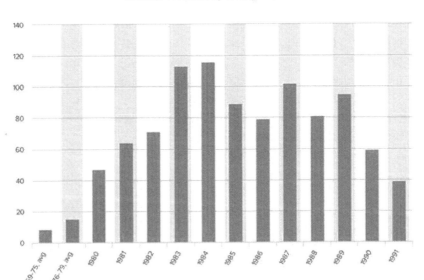

DataHero

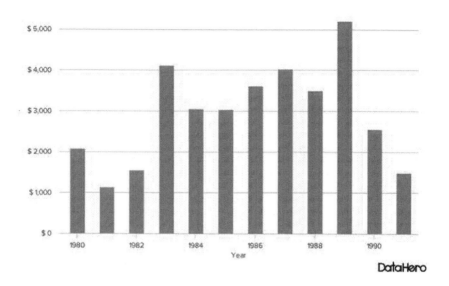

Professors Paul Gompers and Josh Lerner in their book *The Venture Capital Cycle*, published in 2004, said that between 1982 and 1994, firms backed by CVC were more likely to go public than those that were not. On the other hand, CVCs also paid significantly more for their investments. CVCs invested at an average valuation of $28.5 million versus $18.2 million for independent VCs, and so CVC investments did not, in general, outperform those of independent VCs, unless there was a strategic tie between the investing corporation and the start-up, the professors said.

Third Wave of CVC

Then the internet happened, according to Neumann. The catalyst for the 1990s revolution was the invention of the World Wide Web by Tim Berners-Lee in 1990. In January 1993, Marc Andreessen and Eric Bina released the first version of Mosaic, an open-source web browser. Also, in 1993, Europe-based physics laboratory CERN announced the web was free for anyone to use, at just the time when the United States' National Science Foundation

(NSF) freed the academic internet to connect with commercial networks. The 1990s had begun, and high tech was saved, Neumann said.

Consumer adoption of the web created some early winners. AOL went public in 1992; Netscape and nine other internet companies followed suit in 1995. Ten internet initial public offerings (IPOs) in 1995 turned into 18 in 1996, 15 in 1997, and 40 in 1998. In 1999 there were 272 IPOs. Even in 2000 there were 148, despite the stock market crash of March of that year. In 2001 reality sank in, and there were only six internet IPOs, according to data compiled by professor Jay Ritter at the University of Florida.

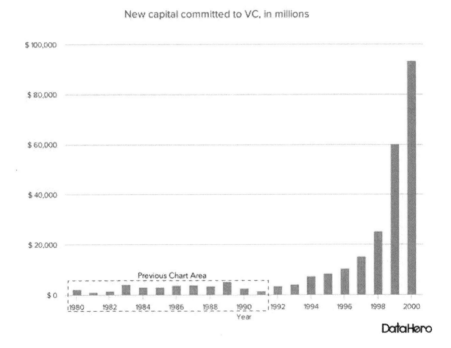

And, again, CVCs followed. Dushnitsky's history notes: "The 1990s experienced the explosion in internet-related technologies and new venture creation, and subsequently a dramatic growth in venture capital investing. Diverse multinational corporations such as News Corp. (EPartners), GlaxoSmithKline (SR One), Texas Instruments (TI Ventures), and Dell

(Dell Ventures) established corporate venture capital funds. By 2000 about 400 CVC programs accounted for approximately 15% of all venture capital investment. As with previous waves, the 2000 crisis in the public markets resulted in a dramatic contraction in venture capital activity and drove many corporations to fold their venturing activities."

Fourth Wave: From Financial Followers to Strategic Leaders

One day, after the global financial crisis and as the implications of Henry Chesbrough's open innovation theory, published in 2003, became better understood, corporations decided venturing was more strategic to their future.

Because of that, they set up CVCs and invested more time, support, and money to find deals, lead them, and use them as part of their innovation toolset helping both portfolio companies and the parent.

Consequently, the venture industry and corporations started to change. The industry became larger and global and part of a merging of private and public capital markets. It became more strategic, while beginning to show financial gains, and corporations started to change as CVC influenced mergers and acquisitions (M&A) and R&D and developed its own professional requirements.

Dushnitsky's history notes:

The [fourth] wave of corporate venture capital has its roots in the mid-2000s...Internet-based ventures (Web 2.0) remain a major investment target, as do other traditional VC target industries such as semiconductors, telecom equipment, biotechnology, and so on. The rapid growth of the AgroTech, CleanTech, and FinTech sectors [covering agriculture, energy, and financial services, respectively] attracted independent and corporate venture capitalists alike. These patterns repeat in terms of the geographical diversity of CVC investment. For instance, a growing fraction of CVCs' portfolios includes ventures based outside the US, including many ventures in developing countries.

Upon further investigation, a few distinct features are notable about the [fourth] wave...An increasing number of corporations view corporate venture capital as a key component of their innovation strategy. Specifically, it is part of a broader transition in corporate R&D strategies; shifting away from an exclusively internal effort and towards embracing external sources of innovations (also known as Open Innovation). As such, corporate venture capital is often viewed as a vehicle to engage and nurture a particularly innovative community: entrepreneurial ventures. The prospect of serving as a pivotal part of a firm's innovation effort results in a fundamental change not only to the role of a CVC program within its parent corporation, but also its contribution to the broader innovation ecosystem.

This broader innovation ecosystem reflects the changing source of innovation from in-house R&D and corporate development teams—the assumption that all the smartest people can work inside one organization—to one where creative ideas are developed among smaller teams.

Small firms' share of R&D spending grew from 4.4 percent in 1981 to 12 percent in 2015, the latest figures released by the US National Science Foundation. These micro-, small-, and medium-sized companies (5 to 249 domestic employees) accounted for 8 percent of sales, employed 12 percent of the 18.9 million who worked for R&D-performing or R&D-funding companies, and employed 23 percent of the 1.5 million employees engaged in business R&D in the United States, the NSF said.

A 2013 study by academics Elisa Alvarez-Garrido and Gary Dushnitsky found that CVC-backed biotechnology ventures are more innovative than their independent VC-backed peers, both in terms of start-ups' scientific publication track record and their patenting output. The evidence suggests that corporate venture capitalists not only select innovative ventures but also nurture them to success. Specifically, the percentage of VC–backed ventures that evolved from a position of innovation-laggards to that of innovation-leaders is only half of that for CVC-backed peers. Further investigation indicates that the benefits to the start-ups are associated with preferential access to corporate advanced facilities, skilled R&D personnel, and manufacturing and regulatory know-how. These are resources that are uniquely characteristic of VC funds that are part of large organizations, even if the parent faces challenges.

In his book *The Vanishing American Corporation: Navigating the Hazards of a New Economy*, Gerald Davis, professor of management and organizations at the University of Michigan, said signs of the corporation's challenges began in the 1980s and 1990s, as the rise of financialization—in which financial services account for a higher share of national income than other sectors—transformed the US economy, and "they learned it does not pay to be big, but it pays to be small." Or it pays at least to work in a distributed way with smaller companies and rely less on financialization.

However, the idea of corporations investing in illiquid, private companies remains controversial. In his 2012 book (recently updated in its second edition), *Doing Capitalism in the Innovation Economy*, William Janeway, a noted academic and venture capitalist at Warburg Pincus through the 1990s and 2000s, warns of corporations paying "premium value for illiquidity."

Effectively, in this Fourth Wave professionalization was evident in particular programs, such as Intel Capital and J&J but was yet to be an industry-wide.

Instead, greater professionalization and institutionalization have really taken off in the past five to seven years in the Fifth Wave, which sees standardization of CVC job descriptions, external benchmarks / data on sector-wide compensation bands, progress around end-to-end investing principles, and commercial advantages via access to parent companies and stewarded relationships.

The macroeconomic shock of the Global Financial Crisis brought the issues into sharper relief but, unlike in prior waves, resulted in a greater number of CVC launches after than before the crisis, according to GCV Analytics, the data research unit of Global Corporate Venturing.

Fifth Wave Reaches New Heights of Professionalism

Corporate venturing's rise this decade with its first near–$100 billion fund raised by SoftBank in 2018 and involvement in venture deals worth more than $100 billion indicates what can be achieved. The smarter groups, such as Didi Chuxing, Tencent, SoftBank, and others identified in chapters 2 through 5, are working out how to combine these into bigger assets to capture the next S-curves of disruptive possibilities.

There are three broad areas for change seen in this Fifth Wave:

1. Impact on the parent
2. Relations with portfolio companies
3. Organizing the corporate venturing unit.

Regarding the first area, CVCs are typically started when external information is valuable, lending support to the hypothesis that firms use CVC to acquire innovation knowledge from start-ups, according to a 2016 paper by Song Ma at the Yale School of Management. CVC programs are terminated when the informational benefit diminishes. This information-acquisition rationale is further supported as CVCs select portfolio companies with similar technological focus but that have a different knowledge base, actively use newly acquired information, and change their human capital to facilitate information acquisition.

While CVC can effect change at the parent over longer cycles, it is also adept at helping shorter-term transitions by improving M&A and R&D efficiency. The Fifth Wave has seen greater understanding of how to run a CVC unit effectively as well as integrate its insights within a wider set of innovation tools.

Bertelsmann is an example of how a Germany-based publisher has used a host of corporate venturing tools, including limited partnership commitments and direct investments, to complement the acquisition of a venture-backed company and build its third main division of education over the past few years.

That Bertelsmann is one of relatively few established media groups to have continued growing against the rise of the digital natives indicates how important venturing and entrepreneurialism are for incumbents.

But the rise of Facebook, Google, and others has, as the Bertelsmann example showed, also encouraged a move beyond core media—selling advertising against content—to diversification into education and beyond. Naspers and Tencent, respectively an old-school media group from apartheid-era South Africa and a China-based messaging app and gaming company, met through corporate venturing. Naspers still owns about a third of Tencent, sold about two percentage points of its holding for about $2 billion, and has been reinvesting in e-commerce start-ups. Together, Naspers and Tencent have grown and reaped the rewards of pushing the boundaries beyond their home countries and sectors even after a portfolio company flotation.

Access to cutting-edge research and business models, support for R&D and M&A teams internally, and financial results from profitable exits means corporate venturing offers plenty to its parent's C-suite of senior executives to pick what suits them best.

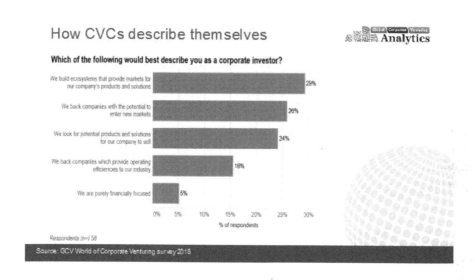

How CVCs describe themselves

Global Corporate Venturing Analytics

Which of the following would best describe you as a corporate investor?

Category	%
We build ecosystems that provide markets for our company's products and solutions	29%
We back companies with the potential to enter new markets	26%
We look for potential products and solutions for our company to sell	24%
We back companies which provide operating efficiencies to our industry	16%
We are purely financially focused	5%

% of respondents

Respondents (n=) 58

Source: GCV World of Corporate Venturing survey 2018

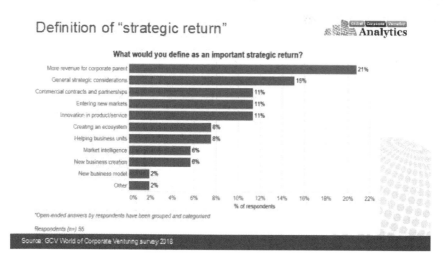

Definition of "strategic return"

Global Corporate Venturing Analytics

What would you define as an important strategic return?

Category	%
More revenue for corporate parent	21%
General strategic considerations	15%
Commercial contracts and partnerships	11%
Entering new markets	11%
Innovation in product/service	11%
Creating an ecosystem	8%
Helping business units	8%
Market intelligence	6%
New business creation	6%
New business model	2%
Other	2%

% of respondents

*Open-ended answers by respondents have been grouped and categorised

Respondents (n=) 55

Source: GCV World of Corporate Venturing survey 2018

Venture Enters the Professional Age

But at the heart of the Fifth Wave is the understanding of the power of an alliance. In the 15 or so years since Henry Chesbrough published in the *Harvard Business Review* the theory of open innovation, the impact has been enormous.

Companies spend more time thinking about the potential changes and disruption happening externally and their responses, even if research-and-development budgets still dwarf the resources allocated to start-ups. Battery Ventures noted Amazon and Alphabet's combined R&D spend in 2017 was $39.2 billion compared to global venture investments in software of $32 billion. Corporate venturing has become more strategic as a way to hedge bets.

It is, therefore, more important to companies, and one signal to this is the increasing numbers of CVC leaders, such as Sue Siegel and Vanessa Colella, being promoted to chief innovation officer or combining the venture role with other innovation tools or functions, such as mergers and acquisitions.

And so corporate venturing has moved from a tool used by a minority of large companies as a competitive advantage over peers to a professional service used by the majority.

Corporate venturing is definitely part of the innovation toolkit of the largest companies

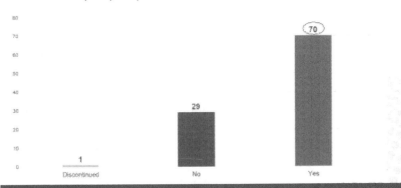

Fortune 100 (2016) companies involved in some corporate venturing*

* Venturing units, LPs in VC funds and/or corporate-backed accelerators and incubators

And they use all the innovation tools accordingly.

This constellation, however, can create duplication and overlap, especially if all the innovation and transformation units report to different people with unclear goals and a lack of metrics. Data provider CB Insights has a nice turn of phrase for this: innovation theater. But for those who approach it the right way, the opportunities are evident, particularly in health care, one of the oldest corporate venturing industries.

Scott Brun, vice president of corporate strategy office at US-based drugs group AbbVie and head of its AbbVie Ventures unit, said: "AbbVie currently operates in the center of the diagram, relying on internal R&D, M&A, and CVC to source our pipeline. For example, over the past two years, two venture investments Alector and Morphic, resulted in business development deals for preclinical neuroinflammatory and fibrosis compounds."

Health care has been a prime example of this pattern. Bruce Booth, veteran investor at Atlas, noted how over the past twenty years, "externally-sourced programs—in-licensed—have delivered almost a two-fold higher rate of success in development versus in-house programs," and by 2015 more than 75 percent of its deals had corporate venture groups as co-investors compared to below 5 percent a decade earlier.

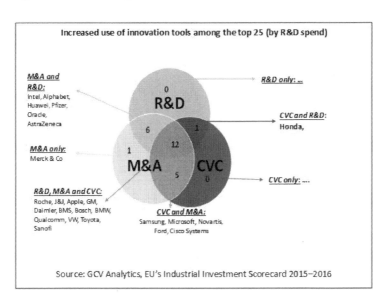

As Gary Dushnitsky said:

Corporate venture capital is associated with a unique impact on advancements in deep innovation. Put differently, the contribution of CVC programs may go beyond adding to the total VC investment in entrepreneurial ventures. The term "deep innovation" describes inventions that are enabled by basic research or scientific breakthrough. It usually entails substantial resources and may take years (10–15), if not decades, to materialize.

The profile of cutting-edge innovation in the energy, life sciences, or space exploration sectors offers some notable illustrations. Most traditional investors, including independent venture capitalists, are deterred by the significant CAPEX [capital expenditure] requirement and undefined time horizons.

Corporate venture capital can make a distinct contribution in such sectors. Consider, for example, recent evidence from the life sciences. The introduction of a cutting-edge drug faces multiple hurdles, including a high level of uncertainty, ever-increasing investment amounts, and longer time to market. Accordingly, the sector attracts fewer independent venture capitalists. Corporate venture capital proves instrumental in driving innovation in the sector.

Corporate Venturing Blurs the Line

It is worth a reminder here of what corporations have brought to the innovation capital ecosystem globally this decade after the global financial crisis started to ebb.

The value of deals done has more than doubled globally between 2012 and 2017 and was primed to climb above the dot-com peak in the United States in 2018, according to the National Venture Capital Association.

This is part of a blurring of public and private capital markets. Whereas up until the dot-com crash around the millennium, most successful private companies tried to list at the earliest opportunity, over the past two decades there has been a growing trend for consolidation, privatization, and slower and fewer IPOs.

In 1997 there were 8,884 companies listed on US stock exchanges. Two decades on, the number has more than halved, even if the aggregate value of the remaining stocks has increased.

The rise in leveraged buyouts by private equity firms and increased mergers and acquisitions among public companies, combined with sophisticated corporate venturing and innovation tools focused on technology changes encouraging scale and cost-cutting, has meant a return to the pre-antitrust era vertical- or horizontal-integrated conglomerates seen a century ago.

In an article for *Atlantic* last year, Frank Partnoy, law professor at the University of California Berkeley, summed up the trend: "Buying big public companies is becoming a sure way to buy lots of small private ones. Many large public companies, including Intel, Johnson & Johnson and Time Warner, have divisions that are explicitly tasked with investing in and sometimes acquiring private companies (some invest in public companies, too). When SoftBank Group, a Japanese conglomerate, created its Vision Fund [in 2017] to invest in technology companies, both private and public, some of the fund's $100bn came from Apple and Qualcomm."

"We believe their new fund will speed the development of technologies which may be strategically important to Apple," Apple company spokesperson Josh Rosenstock told newswire Reuters, confirming in January 2017 its plan to invest $1 billion in the SoftBank Vision fund. Given Apple had $237.6 billion in cash in its fiscal fourth quarter 2016, finding uses for this mountain of cash that could provide financial returns and strategic insights seems reasonable.

For context on SoftBank's Vision fund, the US venture capital industry raised about $350 billion between 2001 and 2010, excluding the $76 billion raised in 2000. That SoftBank alone was involved in about a fifth of US venture deals by value in the third quarter of 2017 indicates the impact it has had. Entrepreneurs are asking for ten times what they might have sought earlier and using the money to develop their own corporate venturing strategies by investing in and acquiring peers in other sectors and geographies.

Media group Tencent and SoftBank's funding of China-based ride-hailing company Didi Chuxing will be perhaps a defining case study of this new world order. It has effectively defeated US peer Uber in China and turned the tables on its erstwhile partner outside North America to be valued more highly and have a more effective partnership model.

What Didi, Tencent, and the others realize is that, as Arjun Sethi puts it, "a moat [a durable competitive advantage] today is simply a temporary buffer that helps a company get ahead of the next innovation cycle."

That is why Tencent effectively reinvests all its profits in corporate venturing, as Jeffrey Li, managing partner at Tencent Investment, said at the inaugural GCV Asia Congress in October 2017.

Corporate Identity Changes

The growth in the importance of intangibles upends economic theory. Arnold King in his blog said:

> Business competition does not consist of building bigger production facilities. It consists of trying to come up with the best strategies for capturing the value of ideas, including the value of spill overs and synergies that come from other people's ideas.
>
> Economic textbooks continue to treat incomes as returns to factors of production, notably labor and capital. Meanwhile, in the real world, incomes at the highest levels are the outcome of management strategy, in mobilizing internal talent and in exploiting the opportunities to use synergy, spill overs, and scalability in the external environment.
>
> As intangible factors increase in importance, strategy matters more, and resource endowments matter less.

A blog by Andrew Chen, head of rider growth for US-based ride-hailing service Uber, which could float this year for up to $120 billion, makes the case that while it has never been cheaper to start a business, to scale it up costs far more in customer acquisition.

Chen said, "All acquisition channels are an efficient market at some point, and this means that companies that monetize better than their competitors (either with higher LTVs [life-time values] or because they enjoy shorter payback periods) will be able to afford a higher CAC [customer acquisition cost] and subsequently out-invest those competitors. In short, better monetization is a competitive advantage for growth."

In this light, therefore, it is interesting to see how firms as diverse as US-listed software provider Microsoft and China-based media group Tencent have developed commercial relationships with portfolio companies.

Corporate Relationships Change

Microsoft was already an investor in Uber, but when it made a huge investment in Indian unicorn Flipkart, it included a provision to switch from Amazon Web Services to Microsoft's Azure cloud-services platform. Similarly, Tencent has partnerships with its portfolio companies to use its' rather than Alibaba's cloud platforms.

The angle for these companies is to look at investments as part of a strategy to win customers to support the parent's main business while also making financial returns from the deal itself. Given the paucity of financial returns generally, such a combination is perhaps uniquely appealing.

It is also working toward a world of, in angel investor Gil Dibner's words, systems of network intelligence—in which a system of intelligence creates incremental value by sharing intelligence across customers.

It could also mark a move beyond CVC. In the GCV annual survey, Mark Sherman, managing director at Telstra Ventures, said:

> Strategic growth investing will become an increasing force in 2017 and in years to come. Corporates will move from under 15% of total ventures dollars invested in the early 2000s to 25% today to over 35% in the next five to 10 years.
>
> Strategic growth investing is different from CVC in that it is larger investment sizes, global orientation, and providing commercial relationships to attract the best entrepreneurs.

This two-way street between corporation and entrepreneur relies on a clear discussion of the value both sides can bring.

The second change in the Fifth Wave, therefore, is looking at the portfolio companies' relationships with CVCs.

From Village Capital

There is a shift from innovation village capital (IVC), with local investors, small deals and VCs always in the lead, just offering capital, maybe some advice and with terms skewed against founders and employees.

Instead, the penny has dropped that entrepreneurs can demand more. Venture is increasingly recognized as a service-orientated profession helping entrepreneurs with their five primary needs of capital, customers, product development, hiring, and an exit, and corporations have opened up their value creation and shareholder returns options.

Wendell Brooks, president of Intel Capital, said in January 2016's Global Corporate Venturing and Innovation Summit that his goal was to find out "what can we do for our portfolio companies, not what can they do for us?"

The democratization of entrepreneurship globally, combined with a wider range of providers of capital than just traditional venture capital— whether angel or crowdfunded, initial coin offerings (ICOs), philanthropic or impact, corporate, university, or government—means that more start-ups have launched and raised money at higher valuations than could have been imagined a dozen years ago, before Apple launched its iPhone, and Facebook connected the Western world.

More broadly, venture capital is getting upended by its own technology. AngelList, for example, is trying to combine platforms that on the one hand bring entrepreneurs together with a wider group of investors and potential employees, and on the other allow these start-ups' products to be recommended and bought by customers. It is a great business model for what is shaping up to be the first mass market age in venture capital and one that will favor artificial-intelligence-enabled decision-making.

As Brian Arthur, an external professor at the Santa Fe Institute and a visiting researcher at the System Sciences Lab at Xerox's Palo Alto Research Centre, wrote for management consultant McKinsey:

> The virtual economy is not just an internet of things, it is a source of intelligent action—intelligence external to human workers.
>
> This shift from internal to external intelligence is important. When the printing revolution arrived in the 15th and 16th centuries it took information housed internally in manuscripts in monasteries and made it available publicly. Information suddenly became

external. It ceased to be the property of the church and now could be accessed, pondered, shared and built upon by lay readers, singly or in unison. The result was an explosion of knowledge, of past texts, theological ideas and astronomical theories. Scholars agree these greatly accelerated the Renaissance, the Reformation, and the coming of science. Printing, argues commentator Douglas Robertson, created our modern world.

Now we have a second shift from internal to external, that of intelligence, and because intelligence is not just information but something more powerful—the use of information—there is no reason to think this shift will be less powerful than the first one. We do not yet know its consequences, but there is no upper limit to intelligence and thus to the new structures it will bring in the future.

The venture industry is democratizing with the rise of angels and ICOs, and the formation of cheaper start-ups changes dynamics for what types of businesses need venture capital. AngelList has a jobs board, Republic for crowdfunding, partnership with CoinList for ICOs and ProductHunt for customers and development. Gust has five hundred thousand funders and seventy thousand investors.

As Roy Bahat, head of Bloomberg Beta, the corporate venturing unit of the financial services technology platform, said, "In our first fund, Bloomberg supported us in creating a different kind of venture fund. We built Bloomberg Beta to treat our founders like we treat Bloomberg's customers, with great care, trust, transparency and a service driven by data."

Or as Yao Xia, executive director for Tencent Investment, winner of Global Corporate Venturing Rising Stars 2017 awards, put it:

Similar to other industries, CVC needs to have a clear understanding and also the good execution on its competitive advantage and differentiate itself from other investors.

Investment is a red [ocean] market, with too many investors and too much money. Although everybody is talking about post-deal management or value-added services to investee companies, but the key thing it can provide is still the same money.

From this perspective, CVC naturally has the capability of differentiation. No matter [whether] it's minority investment or acquisition, CVC should be thinking from the company's perspective, being a trusted friend of the company, and provide its resources and expertise to back the company to grow.

The cottage industry of VC firms being seen as the best providers of capital to fast-growing entrepreneurs has been disrupted. The few remaining successful VCs able to do five or more deals a year and compete with deeper-pocket rivals have stepped up and professionalized.

Venky Ganesan, then-chairman of US trade body the National Venture Capital Association (NVCA), at its joint event with GCV in late October 2016, using data from PitchBook, showed how the VC industry had consolidated, with 211 US firms doing at least five deals a year now compared with 1,000 or more in 2000, and with 60 percent of the money now raised in funds being secured by the top 16 firms.

From a cottage industry of VCs following "pattern recognition" to select former colleagues, fellow university alumni, and sons of friends, the newer breed of venture investor has emerged with the brand, marketing, and support-beyond-money that entrepreneurs want, offered by units that can hire externally experienced and mixed teams.

The future, therefore, is not reaping rewards from information asymmetry and against lifestyle-business peers; it is professional.

Being Smart Capital

In just one news story among dozens each day on innovation capital, the Monetary Authority of Singapore (MAS) in mid-November 2018 said it would launch a $5 billion fund for private market investments. Peter Ong, an MAS board member, at the time said, "There is now a greater recognition among ASEAN [Association of Southeast Asian Nations] companies that private capital is not simply just another source of funds, but also a key form of 'smart capital' that comes with technology, business know-how and networks useful to companies to grow and scale."

But to be smart capital requires listening as well as scenario planning for variable conditions and having resilient sources of funding and commitment. As Union Square's Wilson pointed out five years ago, many start-ups fear that taking corporate money limits their options and comes with strings that could turn away other potential investors—such as a right to buy the company at a later date.

Savvy entrepreneurs often try to bring at least two CVCs into a syndicate to avoid such signaling risks.

Wilson was also concerned that active strategic investments meant CVCs "take a big stake, a board seat, and they make a ton of promises about how much they are going to help the company. These type of investments and relationships have almost universally 'sucked' for our portfolio companies."

In an interview with *Global Corporate Venturing* just after the magazine's launch back in 2010, Reid Hoffman, serial angel investor and cofounder of business networking site LinkedIn (now a partner at VC firm Greylock), warned corporate venturing units to avoid overselling the amount of support they can give portfolio companies.

However, he said his experience at LinkedIn was that corporations, such as software company SAP and media group McGraw-Hill, could be "critical" in helping his entrepreneurial venture build a diversified syndicate of investors.

The top CVCs recognize the need to deliver on their promises. Some do so by asking two executives to support a portfolio company, one specifically to take their corporate parent's view in discussions and the other to see how they might best understand and help the portfolio company. Others manage with one, but the key is to under promise and overdeliver.

After Wilson's comments, Deborah Hopkins, pioneering chief innovation officer (CIO) at US-listed bank Citigroup, said her team acted as the "champion of the entrepreneur" at the large corporation, which otherwise had a tendency to kill more nascent businesses.

She gave the example of Silver Tail Systems, in which Citi invested and made a six-times return in fourteen months after its sale to database provider EMC for about $230 million in 2012. Hopkins said, "We took Silver Tail over the top to the right people, who took its technology inside and piloted it. Our [technology team] already had three companies being tested for similar technology but they loved [Silver Tail] and gave it a very large deal. Unlike VCs, we [corporate venturing units] can help a portfolio scale and do so at Citi volume."

The Silver Tail example is good because it shows how corporate venturers can help effectively open the "right" doors, but then it is down to the portfolio company to prove its worth against the others being tested. The frustration of many entrepreneurs is that the pace of this testing seems slow or the corporate venturers' promises of access and relevance change as the political winds and people shift inside the corporation.

Each corporate is unique and requires an entrepreneur to think about specifically how the syndicate can help for some or all of its five needs and dynamically adjust to the investors as all VCs—corporate, philanthropic, independent, angel, hedge funds, government—bring an angle that needs to be managed.

This management of investors rather than by them is a substantial shift. With the rise of serial entrepreneurs—Amadeus Capital Partners did 17 percent of its deals in the early 2000s with serial entrepreneurs, but this rose to 70 percent in this decade—and a plethora of blogs and content about venture capital, there is greater knowledge inside start-ups about how investors perform.

Exits

And of all those VC-backed companies that went public, on average about three in every ten had received some corporate venture capital backing in previous funding rounds in most years—a higher proportion than the total of CVC-backed start-ups. Academics Thomas Chemmanur, Elena Loutskina, and Xuan Tian studied the flotations from 1980 to 2004, and one of their conclusions was that

> CVC-backed firms [gain] more efficient access to the equity market
> by credibly communicating the true value of firms backed by them
> to three different constituencies:

- First, to IVCs [independent venture capitalists], prompting them to co-invest in these firms pre-IPO.
- Second, to various financial market players such as underwriters, institutional investors and analysts, allowing them to access the equity market at an earlier stage in their lifecycle compared with firms backed by IVCs alone.

- Third, directly to IPO market investors, allowing CVC-backed firms to obtain higher IPO market valuations compared with the valuation of firms backed by IVCs alone.

Tony Palcheck, head of Zebra Ventures, for the GCV exits study published in late 2016 said, "The top five companies in the S&P 500 were backed by venture capital investors, and all of them do some type of corporate VC investing. The fact that they are the most valuable companies in the world implies that they know what they are doing from a financial return perspective. The fact that they themselves are investing money in start-ups implies that they believe they can create value in start-ups—as well as extract that value."

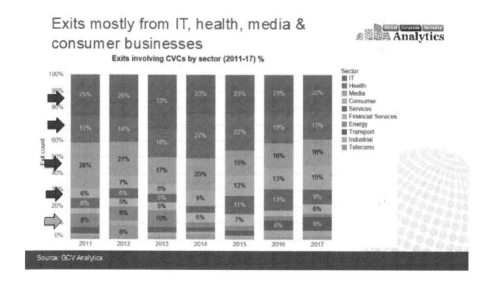

Exits mostly from IT, health, media & consumer businesses

Exits involving CVCs by sector (2011-17) %

Industrial & energy business late to exit

Global Corporate Venturing **Analytics**

Average time to exit (years) for CVC-backed companies

Exit Type	Sector	2013	2014	2015	2016	2017
Acquisitions	Consumer		2.4	2.9	2.9	3.7
	Energy	2.4	2.5	2.8	6.2	6.4
	Financial Services	1.4	3.1	1.8	1.7	4.4
	Health	2.7	2.4	2.6	2.7	5.2
	Industrial	1.8		6.4	2.7	2.0	4.1
	IT	2.8	1.8	2.3	3.1	4.4
	Media	1.2	1.9	3.7	2.6	5.3
	Services	2.3	1.5	2.8	2.0	4.5
	Telecoms	2.5	1.6		4.5	4.0
	Transport	1.9	2.0	2.7	2.9	3.1
IPOs	Consumer	2.0	1.9	1.9		4.5
	Energy	2.0	3.0	2.9	4.6	
	Financial Services	1.2	2.8	2.4		3.8
	Health	1.3	2.5	2.1	2.7	3.7
	Industrial					3.5
	IT	1.8		2.9	4.0	5.6
	Media	2.0	2.7		4.0	
	Services		3.7		2.4	
	Telecoms	3.4			5.0	
	Transport		4.1			

Exit Type
■ Acquisitions
■ IPOs

*Average time since first recorded corporate-backed round

Source: GCV Analytics

Fifth Wave Impact on M&A

M&As as a way to access external innovation is well understood, judging by Lora Dimitrova's paper, "Strategic Acquisitions by Corporate Venture Capital Investors," as it can in short order change a business' sales and staff makeup. What is recently becoming clearer is that firms with a CVC program make a greater number of acquisitions.

Acquirers earn positive and significant returns on average when they acquire start-ups outright in which they have no prior equity investment. CVC investors are indeed better acquirers, but only in years in which they are actively investing in start-ups. Information sharing is important.

A 2018 paper, "How Transparent are Firms About Their Corporate Venture Capital Investments?" found that future sales contribution from acquisitions is higher for firms with a CVC program, and they are less likely to overpay for them. These results suggest that a parent firm having a CVC program tends to have more potential acquisition targets to consider and, among the acquisitions that are made, there is a higher likelihood for increased sales but not a higher likelihood for failure.

But acquisition returns are significantly lower (and significantly negative) when acquirers purchase start-ups in which they have a prior equity investment, although dedicated units are again significantly less likely to overpay.

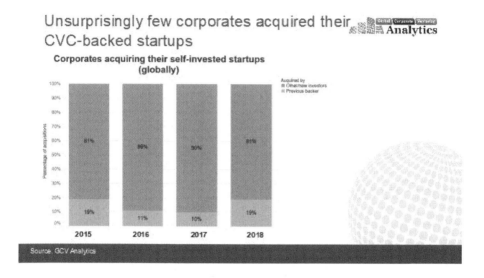

Unsurprisingly few corporates acquired their CVC-backed startups

Corporates acquiring their self-invested startups (globally)

Source: GCV Analytics

Alphabet, the parent conglomerate of the Google search engine, is the heaviest acquirer of portfolio companies from its corporate venture unit, GV (one of the most active CVCs globally and one of a number of similar CVC units run by Alphabet), formerly Google Ventures. GV made six acquisitions in the three years to the end of 2016, according to GCV Analytics.

Alphabet has acquired at least sixty-three companies since the start of 2014 to late 2016, according to its Wikipedia page, indicating that less than a tenth of the acquisitions in this period were sourced from its corporate venturing unit, even including its purchases of GV-backed Skybox, Urban Engines, Appurify, and Nest, among others.

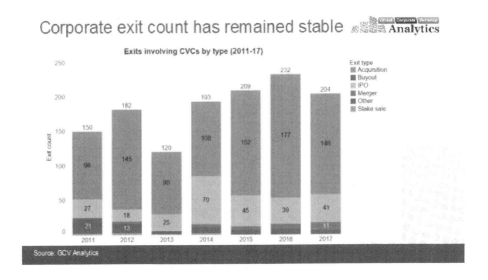

Capital Expands

And with greater competition for deals from investors as money supply has expanded, the rewards for entrepreneurial success become clear.

There has been an infusion of capital as US money supply has exploded over the past decade—M0 has broadly trebled since 2008—and "a low interest rate environment means a low cost of capital, which means yield is hard to find for cash," and thus the flow into private markets. Global debt rose to a record $237 trillion in 2017, or about 318 percent of gross domestic product (GDP), according to the Institute of International Finance.

Balance sheet sizes have become a moat. In addition to technology, network effects, and expertise, a start-up's cash position is a competitive advantage. Imagine two start-ups in the same space with similar funding. The one that can raise a $250 million round from a later-stage mega-fund suddenly has a huge and difficult-to-assail advantage in the five forces driving start-up valuations today, according to Tomasz Tunguz.

...Today's Top 20 Worldwide Internet Leaders *Today* =
USA @ 11...China @ 9

Public / Private Internet Companies, Ranked by Market Valuation (5/29/18)

Rank 2018	Company	Region	Market Value ($B) 5/29/13	5/29/18
1)	Apple	USA	$418	$924
2)	Amazon	USA	121	783
3)	Microsoft	USA	291	753
4)	Google / Alphabet	USA	288	739
5)	Facebook	USA	56	538
6)	Alibaba	China	--	509
7)	Tencent	China	71	483
8)	Netflix	USA	13	152
9)	Ant Financial	China	--	150
10)	eBay + PayPal*	USA	71	133
11)	Booking Holdings	USA	41	100
12)	Salesforce.com	USA	25	94
13)	Baidu	China	34	84
14)	Xiaomi	China	--	75
15)	Uber	USA	--	72
16)	Didi Chuxing	China	--	56
17)	JD.com	China	--	52
18)	Airbnb	USA	--	31
19)	Meituan-Dianping	China	--	30
20)	Toutiao	China	--	30
	Total		$1,429	$5,788

Source: Mary Meeker's Internet Trends 2018 report, Kleiner Perkins Caufield & Byers

Corporates have resources to make a difference

$ USD 22 Trillion

in Cash, Cash Equivalents and Short Term Investments on balance sheets

 ▲ 5.3% CAGR over the last 5 years

Regional breakdown $ USD Bn

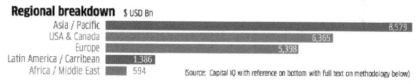

Asia / Pacific	8,579
USA & Canada	6,365
Europe	5,398
Latin America / Carribean	1,386
Africa / Middle East	594

(Source: Capital IQ with reference on bottom with full text on methodology below)

The top fifty holders of cash account for $1.08 trillion (per Moody's) and 90 percent have a CVC operation in-house or indirectly, according to Global Corporate Venturing.

Top 5 Cash-Rich US Companies & bosses/founders

Company	Total ($bn)	Industry	CVC
Apple (Laurene Jobs Powell $20bn))	285*	Technology	managed by KPCB, Softbank Vision Fund
Microsoft (co-founders $110bn)	131.2	Technology	M12
Google (CEO $55bn)	86.3	Technology	GV, CapitalG, Gradient, Google Assistant
Cisco (Ex-CEO $1bn)	71.8	Technology	Cisco Investments
Oracle (ex-chr $61.8bn)	58.2	Technology	balance sheet

Source: *Moody's Financial Metrics' projection November 2017, otherwise 2016. Global Corporate Venturing

Regional Growth

And sectors tend to know few borders. As well as providing enough support to allow companies to stay private for longer and continue to grow and scale, corporations have encouraged the globalization of entrepreneurship beyond the United States by investing outside of their home country or even the main VC centers, such as Silicon Valley.

Silicon Valley Bank's fourth quarter 2018 report noted that the next wave of disruptive US venture investing could come from regions outside Silicon Valley, driven by the customer-focused entrepreneurs locating near the F500 "old guard."

Where Will Venture Head Next?

As technology becomes vital across all sectors, the next wave of disruption may well emerge from customer-focused companies situated near the old guard. Regions like the South, Southeast and Midwest are home to a greater share of Fortune 500 companies than U.S. venture investment.

Fortune 500 Companies and Venture Funding by Region (% of U.S.)

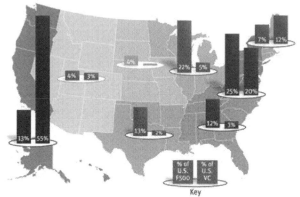

States with Largest Gap between Fortune 500 vs. Venture Funding[1]

State	F500	VC	Gap
Texas	10%	2%	7.6%
Illinois	7%	2%	5.3%
Ohio	5%	1%	4.4%
Virginia	5%	1%	3.9%
New Jersey	4%	1%	3.5%
Connecticut	4%	1%	3.0%
Michigan	3%	0%	3.0%
Minnesota	4%	1%	2.9%
Pennsylvania	4%	1%	2.7%
Georgia	3%	1%	2.4%

Source: Silicon Valley Bank

About half of CVCs invest in more than one country

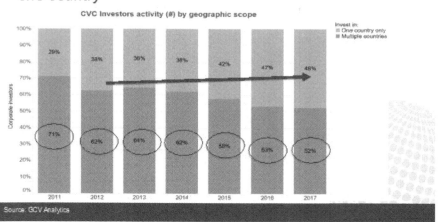

Source: GCV Analytics

Fewer than three out of every ten VC firm are international in scope, according to PitchBook data, while more than half of CVCs invest across borders, GCV Analytics found. And this approach opens up the world to greater competition.

Asia's Growth Eclipses the United States

In investment bank Goldman Sachs's Venture Capital Horizons note in August, Heath Terry said, "While corporate venture capital has been a major driver of growth in venture as an asset class globally, nowhere has that been more evident than Asia, where Alibaba, Baidu, JD.com, and Tencent have followed the lead of SoftBank, creating massive ecosystems of venture investments under their umbrellas. Nearly every major private company in China has at least one of those five companies as an investor, and the level of influence these ecosystems have in steering the development of new technologies and business models is unprecedented."

China had overtaken the United States for CVC back in 2017, according to GCV Analytics, and, as of the end of June 2018, Asia represented 47 percent of the total VC funding over the trailing twelve-month period, surpassing North America (41 percent share) for the second consecutive quarter, Goldman Sachs said.

Taking as a starting point probably the most comprehensive list of such unicorns (companies worth at least $1 billion) in China—the 108 tracked by China Money Network (CMN) as of August 28, 2018—more than 90 percent of them appeared from public records to have at least one corporate venturing investor in the syndicate, according to GCV Analytics. GCV Analytics found that nearly half of CMN's list of Chinese unicorns, 46, had at least one of the BATJs as an investor, led by Tencent, which last year said it had backed 100 unicorns—companies worth at least $1billion—out of 600 it had invested in over the past decade.

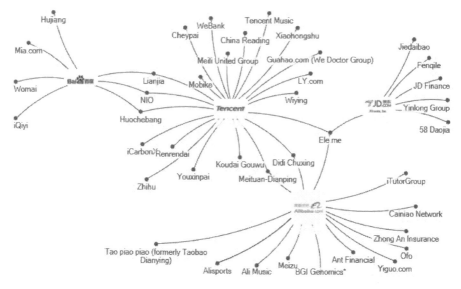

Source: GCV Analytics

Corporate Venturing Leaders

But while Tencent and others have inside a decade reached the tops of the venture industry, for others the challenges to develop a successful unit or approach to entrepreneurs remain acute.

As with the broader VC industry, there is a persistence among the top corporations. The top 20 percent of the industry are responsible for the most deals; almost all have at least a decade's track record, and some, such as Johnson & Johnson, stretch back to the 1970s.

Many corporate investors, however, are episodic. Only about a third of these investors can be called "regular" (i.e., they have participated in eleven or more deals for a given period of time).

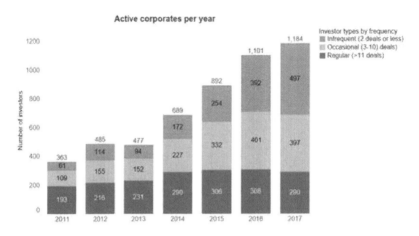

Source: GCV Analytics

The top 20 percent of CVCs—such as GCV Leadership Society Luminary members Intel Capital, Tencent, Capital One, Merck Global Health Innovations, GE Ventures, and Johnson & Johnson Innovation–JJDC—are responsible for about 85 percent of deal flow, according to GCV Analytics. A fifth of CVCs—often the same ones—also generated an annual rate of return of 30 percent or higher, according to GCV's annual survey.

GCV Analytics tracked 1,354 deals worth an estimated $85.3 billion in the first half of 2018, of which $66 billion—77 percent—were deployed in 145 deals that were $100 million or larger.

For context, in the twelve months to the end of March 2014, there were forty-seven deals of at least $100 million, forty-one of which included corporate venturing units in their investment histories, before the numbers started to shoot up in the second-quarter that year with thirty-two large deals of at least $100 million that raised nearly $7.4 billion overall, according to Global Corporate Venturing's analysis and a GCV Symposium keynote address.

The same sorts of names crop up in many of these large rounds, such as GCV Leadership Society members SoftBank and Tencent. Probably unsurprisingly, therefore, during the first half of 2018, $42.3 billion of the $66 billion GCV Analytics tracked went to China-based companies. In comparison, $15.3 billion went to US-based emerging businesses.

These are the leaders in the industry, but their good work and professionalism risks being drowned by the noise of less thoughtful peers doing a handful of deals and then retreating, leaving entrepreneurs confused and giving competitors for quality investments a marketing edge.

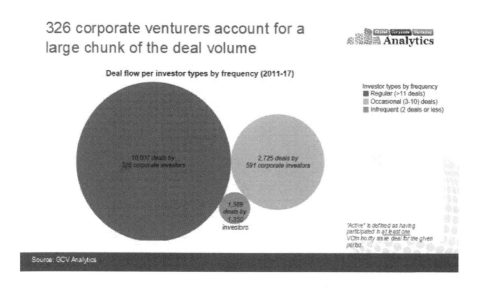

326 corporate venturers account for a large chunk of the deal volume

Deal flow per investor types by frequency (2011-17)

Investor types by frequency
Regular (>11 deals)
Occasional (3-10) deals)
Infrequent (2 deals or less)

10,807 deals by 326 corporate investors

2,725 deals by 591 corporate investors

1,509 deals by 1,350 investors

"Active" is defined as having participated in at least one VCM holdty stake deal for the given period

Source: GCV Analytics

Longevity Requires Adaptability

With longevity comes the need for flexibility. In an interpretation of naturalist Charles Darwin's *Origin of the Species*, Leon Megginson writes, "It is not the strongest species that survive, nor the most intelligent, but the ones most responsive to change."

For his GCV Rising Stars award last year, Pär Lange, founding partner at phone operator Swisscom's ventures unit, summed it up:

> I think Swisscom Ventures itself is my biggest success. While many other CVCs have been victims of reorganizations and strategy changes, we have managed to develop and improve our model continuously over the last 10 years without any disruption.

The fact that we have brought strategic value to Swisscom in combination with having a portfolio with good returns has been key to our success.

Naspers, a South Africa–based media company that invested in Tencent a few years after its formation, is now arguably more of a diversified e-commerce, media and education company given some of its recent investments. Its valuation might still fail to include all its underlying assets but compared with its R132.5 million (now $10.7 million) market cap at its April 1994 flotation, Naspers at R1.34 trillion now is exponentially more valuable.

The importance of venture to strategic decision-making means one thing is clear: there will be more activity. For the GCV Powerlist 100 nomination process in 2018, Bob van Dijk, CEO of Naspers, said, "Naspers looks to invest in entrepreneurs around the world that are building leading businesses addressing big societal needs. Naspers Ventures, led by Larry Illg, has invested in several new segments for us doing just that. The new areas of investment include education, food, health and agriculture, and continued investments in some of these segments will help to build the future of Naspers."

And Diversity

To do so also requires empathy, or high so-called emotional quotient, and communication skills to metaphorically kiss all the frogs among the entrepreneurs to find those capable of transmuting into unicorns, tackle the inevitable politics at the corporate venturing unit itself, and manage the often vast, sprawling and inward-looking business units at the parent as well as senior C-suite executives sitting in judgment on investment committees or deciding whether to continue funding versus other priorities.

Certainly, compared to independent VCs, many corporate venturing units address these needs with teams that demonstrate more racial, gender and ethnic diversity.

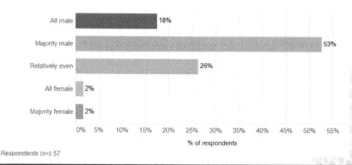

Gender ratios in CVCs still very unequal   Analytics

What is the male-to-female ratio in your team?

All male	18%
Majority male	53%
Relatively even	26%
All female	2%
Majority female	2%

% of respondents

Respondents (n=) 57

Source: GCV World of Corporate Venturing survey 2018

The Future

And diversity will matter. In advising on our last theme, "Standing on the Shoulders of Giants: Going beyond Capital," for the GCV Symposium in London on May 22–23 2018, Sir Ronald Cohen—founder of the British Private Equity and Venture Capital Association, Apax Partners, Bridges Ventures, Social Finance, and Big Society Capital, and chairman of the Global Steering Group for Impact Investment and the Portland Trust—said the twenty-first-century shift in mindset is one from looking simply at risk and reward to finding the appropriate blend of risk, return, and impact.

If investing is intentionality with measurement of impact, then the slightly disparate worlds of traditional venture investing and impact investing will start to combine. This creates opportunities for new regions and investment models.

The global scope for innovation remains broad once you take into account geographic, gender, and ethnic considerations, and with more than $200 trillion of financial assets in stocks, bonds and other securities, there is plenty of capital available. White male graduates from Stanford might be tapped out as a source, but there are others with good ideas and ability to run scalable businesses and corporate venturing units.

When John Doherty, then-head of Verizon Ventures, nominated Merav Rotem Naaman, managing director at Verizon Ventures Israel, for the GCV Rising Stars 2018 awards, it was only a few months after Verizon had acquired AOL and she and her team at its Nautilus corporate venturing unit had been formally integrated.

And it is worth quoting Rotem Naaman's thoughts about why she had done well at some length:

> There are many reasons why Israel has become "the Start-up Nation"—a small country that is virtually an island, where the vast majority of the population are recent immigrants, where 18-year-old kids have to serve in the military and take on responsibilities that for most people take decades.
>
> I grew up in this environment idolizing my parents, grandparents and the other pioneers who lost everything in the World Wars and came to Israel to rebuild their lives and a new home. Asking questions and trying and failing were the norms; entrepreneurship was everywhere and in everything. And in me.
>
> From a very early age I was determined to create my own path, to define my own destiny and to take advantage of the opportunities that life presented, which were not necessarily part of what being raised as a female in a small orthodox community expected of me.
>
> So, I left my community, first to serve in the military and then to attend university where I studied law. During my studies I took a year off to hike across South America and came back smarter, stronger, more open minded and with the courage to take big risks.
>
> I have brought this to my career where I challenged myself to take on the tough jobs and make big moves, from leaving a successful legal career in Israel to attend Harvard Business School, to starting Nautilus, AOL's investment arm in Israel, and now leading Verizon Ventures' first investment group that's located outside the US.

My success is also rooted in the people that I surround myself with both at work and in my personal life. Good teams, happy teams, diverse teams along with my vibrant family and friends are the fuel that keeps me going.

This might help explain why Israelis appear to be the most overrepresented by number of Rising Stars as a proportion of population. Success comes from the environment and people that surround them, but it is also an explanation for the industry's success—Israelis are smart, interested, and willing to help others.

And while diversity can bring complexity and require greater investment in time and effort to understand, it also brings to light greater opportunities, less groupthink and the chance to make the world a better place.

Historian Melvin Kranzberg's first law states: "Technology is neither good nor bad—nor is it neutral." This seems increasingly relevant even after thirty years.

The future is, in many ways, made by those who fund it. Smart corporate venturers are an increasingly important part of this future, but how to get there requires understanding the evolution and changes they go through at different stages of their development—the subject of the next chapters—as well as the broader economic and societal backdrop that provides the meta perspective of the five waves seen so far.

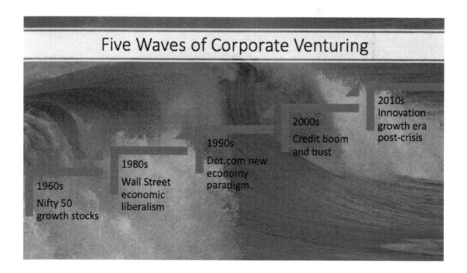

Five Waves of Corporate Venturing

1960s
Nifty 50 growth stocks

1980s
Wall Street economic liberalism

1990s
Dot.com new economy paradigm

2000s
Credit boom and bust

2010s
Innovation growth era post-crisis

CHAPTER 2

Welcome to the Fifth Wave: A Frame for High-Performance CV Program Development

As discussed in chapter 1, for more than half a century corporate venturing (CV) has undergone massive changes that track with the growth and evolution of venture capital (VC), in a series of "waves" disrupted by economic downturns. Many speculate that we are currently on the verge of yet another downturn. In the past, market corrections and economic downturns triggered the end of a cycle for corporate venturing programs: they were often among the early victims of cutbacks or dissolution when parent companies responded to economic uncertainties by retrenching and reorganizing, with more near-term focus on cash conservation and core business profitability.

Will this time be different? What are the key factors that frame this new reality and improve the odds of ongoing, uninterrupted CV program operations? Will CV programs succeed in a continuous delivery of impact that *really does matter*—to parents, portfolio companies, and partners alike?

What can be learned from CV professionals currently accelerating their programs' strategic impact and financial performance in ways that have persuaded parents of their essential value and vital role in corporate strategy, shaping paths and options for corporate growth and staying power? And can these learnings translate to improvements in other companies' programs?

The Environmental Realities Facing CV Programs Have Not Changed

Given the velocity, ubiquity of technology, and market disruption that mark today's environment for corporate venturing, these are the CV program design realities that have *not* _changed, and that make corporate venturing inherently difficult to do well, and in a lasting way:

- **One size has never fit all.**

   There is no one "canonical" corporate venturing program design, given the range of parent company priorities, environments, and differences by sectors; corporate sizes, shapes, and cultures; and geographies. Before the professionalization of the CV practice, program/team design was largely ad hoc, unpredictable, and unrepeatable across companies. Now there is a growing population of experienced CV professionals who understand that customization/adaptation to the parent environment is a vital part of the vision that drives development of the CV program plan/charter, and shapes mutual expectations for impact that "counts."

- **Strategic or financial performance? It's always been both. And it's always been "muddy."**

   Corporations have typically expected from their CV programs a blend of strategic and financial performance, adjusted by parent-specific priorities and lead times. Parent companies have been driven to tap new types of external innovation that strategically leverage the core and create diversified paths to growth and competitive staying power. But the means of framing, measuring, and evaluating the strategic value/relevance of CV programs and portfolios have remained an inexact art, difficult to "crack" in any standard cross-sector way.

   As a result, CV program financial objectives and evidence of VC-like process rigor/discipline historically have served as risk reducers and controls on these "high risk," unfamiliar types of investing and partnering. Financial returns have been categorized as CV participation "table stakes" and returns as a means of offsetting costs and helping to justify program continuance.

With the Fifth Wave comes the promise of finally "cracking the code," with better means of understanding and measuring strategic and financial performance. It starts with acknowledging impediments:

o **Corporate "antibodies" that threaten CV program operation are natural, permanent fixtures of healthy parent company environments.**

Corporate "antibodies" can prove serious impediments to successful implementation of CV program plans and portfolio company "landing spots" and commercial relationships with parents. Experienced CV teams know these "antibodies" must be understood, anticipated, and managed, as an ongoing part of the CV program and parent alignment and collaboration.

o **Corporate changes happen cyclically, without warning, and in varying degrees of severity.**

Happening as frequently as every couple of years, corporate changes are a fact of life for CV programs and teams, from management changes/business reorganizations, to more dramatic events like corporate strategy changes, business redirections, M&A, or down cycle restructuring. All come without warning and have the potential to derail CV program strategy and momentum, fracture CV program/ parent alignments, and jeopardize CV teams' abilities to deliver value and maintain the positions expected by outside portfolio companies and partners.

This is the predictable "baseline," the wholly natural reality for CV programs and their parent companies, dynamics around which corporate venturing teams must consistently "duck and weave" if their programs are to survive— and not just in their start-up phase, but continuously, throughout program expansion and scale.

What's Different for CV Programs Now?

Many external impediments to quality CV program development have been ameliorated by:

- Greater practitioner adoption of "end-to-end" CV investing principles
- Professionalization of CV practices, programs, and teams
- External recognition of the vital position of savvy strategic investors and their ability to bring strategic and commercial value "beyond the investment" to portfolio companies, as well as to syndicate and business development partners

The biggest impediments that remain are, ironically, those associated with the corporate parent. Enduring CV programs will experience the full spectrum of corporate changes/shifts over time. These are predictably disruptive to CV program development and impact delivery. For a CV program to continue to be strategically relevant and impactful for the parent from one day to the next requires the greatest degree of program/team strategic and operational agility and adaptability.

While CV practice and program professionalization have contributed to the "mainstreaming" of corporate venturing and its recognition as an important but differentiated component of the parent's innovation toolkit, there are still key dependencies:

- Parent desire to see indicators of program performance in three years or less. (Typical corporate "patience cycle" aligns with lead time to next reorganization.)
- Recognition that "standard operating procedures" between CV program and parent are inherently different from one another and will remain so (although CV programs are acknowledged as providing unique paths/options to future growth).
- CV program benefits/contributions must always be seen to outweigh the internal operating frictions and increased risk/exposures to the parent, particularly in regulated industries. Dips in program performance and strategic relevance leave CV programs/teams highly vulnerable. (CV program relevance must justify "exception basis" handling required for its management.)

A Refresh on the Basics of Corporate Venturing

The pace of technology and market disruptions continues to accelerate. These disruptions both threaten and create tremendous upside potential for parents who know how to participate in their commercialization and new market creation. But this has also created a sea change in awareness that no one company is, by itself, adequately equipped to drive this unprecedented level of change to its full fruition without the collaboration of other like-minded, complementary investment and business development partners. In parallel, board and C-suite recognition of the importance of venturing and innovation to corporate strategy and staying power has led to the reshaping of higher-level executive management roles to lead these essential corporate efforts and the recruitment of veteran CV&I professionals for broader, higher-level executive management positions, such as chief innovation officer.

Characteristics of Fifth Wave Corporate Venturing Programs

- **Recognition of innovation partnering criticality and required skill set**

    High performers "institutionalize" this Fifth Wave shift from vertical to horizontal thinking to access new levels of opportunities— global, horizontal in application, cross-segment, cross-industry. This eliminates historical "silos" and leverages the inherent power in global innovation ecosystems to help drive change, targeting customer-centric opportunities and applications in adjacent markets, as well as platforms that can spawn multiple businesses and breakaway ventures.

- **Understanding of the unique and powerful role of CV programs in the corporate innovation portfolio**

    The increasingly mainstream role of most corporate venturing programs is to address innovation opportunities that go beyond established business enhancements and that fall within the "red circle" in figure 2.

    As opposed to established businesses standard operating procedures (e.g., near-term product roadmaps, product development processes, quarter-to-quarter profitability/reporting), red circle investments/collaborations must be managed according to new venture

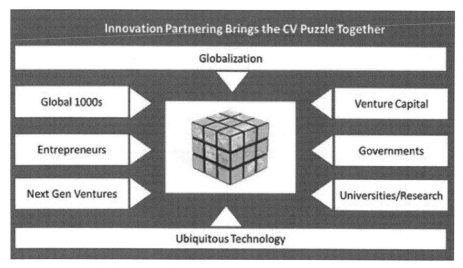

Figure 1: Innovation Partnering brings the CV puzzle together (© Bell Mason Group 2011)

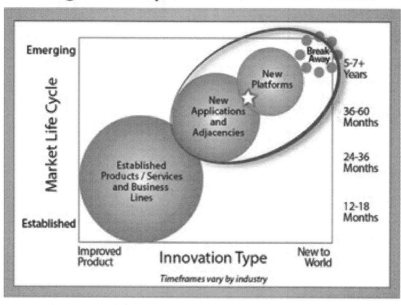

Figure 2: Spectrum of innovation, and the "sweet spot" for leveraging CV
know-how and optimizing parent company advantages (© Bell Mason Group 2011)

creation principles and entrepreneurial ways of working. This predicts the need for very different types of governance, risk management, operating processes, and ways of gauging strategic/financial performance.

Figure 2 also suggests a simple way to map integrated, balanced portfolio roadmaps, tuned to meet CV program development goals and adjusted for a parent's particular objectives and expectations for lead-time-to-returns and impact delivery. The star indicates the "sweet spot" for many corporates, where they have the best opportunity to bring their brands, market positions, and resources to bear in commercializing products and creating markets.

- **An end-to-end investing approach drives both financial performance and strategic impact**

  High-performer CV programs are adopting and formalizing an "end-to-end" investing approach, with an eye toward demonstrating both the financial performance and the end-game strategic impact that will persuade parents of their continuous value to the company. (See figure 3.)

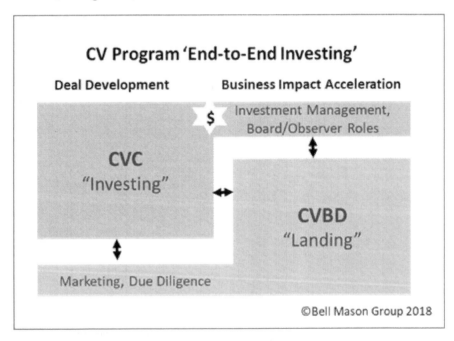

Figure 3: End-to-end investing (sourcing to landing spot)

This end-to-end approach includes new formalization of key elements and tools designed to deliver on timelier and more impactful parent/portfolio engagement. For example:

o   Dedicated portfolio development/corporate venture BD (CVBD) teams and integrated processes
o   High-performance portfolio and innovation partnering programs (internal and external)
o   An up-leveled portfolio and performance management function (tracking and reporting)

- **CV program structured as a multifaceted, mainstream element of the corporate innovation toolkit**

    While corporates have doubled down on innovation as a priority in driving growth and industry leadership, corporate venturing has professionalized and defined a distinctive end-to-end investing approach, designed from the outset to deliver value-boosting landing spots and commercial opportunities for its portfolio companies and ventures with parents and parents' customers and partners.

    High-performer programs with specialist senior-level teams often bring together a range of corporate venturing flavors/dedicated functions as well as alignment with other corporate innovation enablers such as M&A, Strategic Alliances, and JV/Licensing. (See figure 4.)

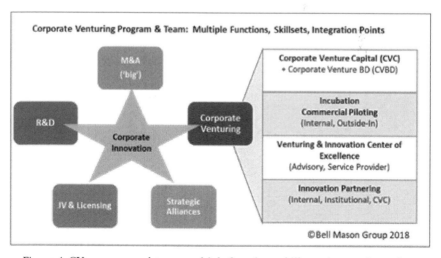

Figure 4: CV program and team: multiple functions, skill sets, integration points

- **Specialist CV team navigates and connects two vastly different worlds (harder than VC investing)**

    So, what is at the core of the corporate venturing program operation that makes it so complex to implement successfully? CV programs/teams must balance on the knife edge between the parent company and the external innovation ecosystem. They must perform flawlessly in two diametrically different worlds that operate according to very different rules, governance structures, clock rates, and expectations. CV teams know that all stakeholders in these complex arrangements must benefit if they are to succeed, investment by investment, project by project, and with multipliers of portfolio value. (See figure 5.)

    The development of trusted access and the ongoing quality of senior relationships in critical "inside/outside" infrastructures are essential CV program /platform enablers and channels for "impact" implementation. Doing this well requires a sophisticated team of dedicated, senior CVC/CVBD professionals who are agile and dynamically adaptive network builders and problem solvers and can seamlessly move from deal sourcing to end-to-end portfolio company landings and commercial relationships.

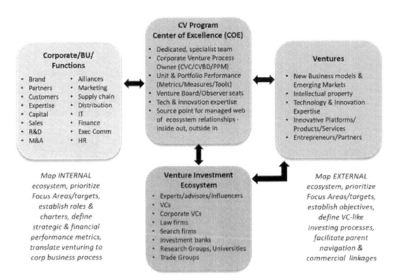

Figure 5: A CV team faces a much more complex world and set of performance requirements than VC counterparts (© **Bell Mason Group** 2011)

A Framework for Fifth Wave CV Program Analysis and Planning: Five Dimensions, Three Maturation Phases

As CV professionals know well, there are many moving parts and degrees of "3D complexity" involved in developing and syncopating all the pieces of the CV program puzzle—many things that must come together in the right ways at the right times, all customized to be adaptable and extensible in specific parent company environments.

Three fundamental questions inform Fifth Wave programs:

1. **How important** is this program to corporate strategy and optional paths to staying power?
2. **How fast** is trajectory to performance indicators and impact?
3. **How resilient** is the program/team—is it able to remain agile/adaptive and intact across the spectrum of corporate changes and shifts?

Bell Mason Group developed a model that started from an embedded cross-sector, cross-industry analysis of what is the same/what is different in successful program development and distilled it into a higher-level framework and set of design guidelines that can be applied to all:

- **Five operational dimensions**—functional categories/elements and acceleration levers common to all programs

Dimension	Contents	Levers for Acceleration
Charter	• Program objectives • Investment strategy and models • Funding • Lead times/ performance expectations	• Vision-driven program and execution roadmap • Expansion of financial tools and funding access (ability to "make markets")
Process	• Legal structure and governance • End-to-end investing platform • Portfolio management	• Institutionalized integration of investing (CVC) and portfolio development (CVBD) • Streamlined governance, performance reporting

MASON · ARRINGTON · MAWSON

Dimension	Contents	Levers for Acceleration

Team	• Leader
	• Professionalized roles and experience
	• Team strategy/ structure
	• Recruiting and retention
	• Strategic outsourcing/ specialty functions
		• Exceptional HR treatment of CV program:
		  – External recruitment of senior CVC/CVBD specialists
		  – Competitive "CV track"— roles, compensation, titles/bands, career paths
		• Alignment of CVBD team and Parent collaborators (sponsors, "catchers," SMEs, etc.)
		• Strategic outsources—CV specialist service provider network: e.g., accounting, legal, search, compensation, deal data, innovation strategy/investment focus area landscaping

Innovation Partnering	• Internal stakeholder network • External ecosystem development and positioning	• Ecosystem vision for execution against strategic focus areas, delivery of value to parent • Priority BU/functional champions and working agreements, internal wiring to drive portfolio collaboration and strategic/ commercial value • "Ecosystem syndicates"— complementary investors/ partners to diversify risk, reduce lead time to value
Performance	• Strategic: delivery on charter objectives, business impact • Financial: Don't lose $; VC metrics, transparent rigor, discipline, exits, and M&A	• Clarity and agreement with parent re: appropriate mix of financial performance and strategic impact metrics, KPIs • Blueprint for agile, extensible CV platform

Dimension	Contents	Levers for Acceleration
	• Operational: CVC platform development and quality • CV marketing/comms function: business model enablement, CV positioning/brand enhancement	• Sophisticated marketing/ comms function—proactive internal and external network development/ relationship management; tracking of/influence on perception of program performance and value

- **Three Program Maturation Phases**—characterized by critical, incremental development milestones, evidence of progress, and indicators of programs beginning to run off track

Phase Characteristics	Phase 1: Years 0–3 (Start-up)	Phase 2: Years 4–6 (Expansion)	Phase 3: Years 7–9+ (Resiliency)
Description	Foundational, vision-driven design, and first build-out of CV program platform and core team	Test of readiness for scale: Core team, "CV platform," early program performance indicators, and envisioned options and tools for expansion	Enduring mainstream program and valued contributor to corporate parent growth and innovation strategy
The Goal	Earn respect with early indicators of being "on track" with professional CV program	Obtain parent commitment for program step-up/ continuation— funding, people, operating reach	Demonstrate long-term CV program resiliency in the face of constant change
Focus	Accelerate CV program design and development	Refine portfolio strategy and options/tools for program expansion	Broaden charter to address new sectors/ geos, "market maker" tools and opportunities

Phase Characteristics	Phase 1: Years 0–3 (Start-up)	Phase 2: Years 4–6 (Expansion)	Phase 3: Years 7–9+ (Resiliency)
Operating Style	<u>Testing while doing</u>: Build, test, refine, operationalize initial CV platform	Institutionalization: Dedicated professional team, extensible end-to-end investing platform	Optimization: CV platform tuned for scale and adaptability; team structure/processes support large scale investing and impactful parent engagement
Performance	Start the "clock" for speed of program development, quality and path to performance	Demonstration of program momentum and internal/external credibility	Robust portfolio management function tracks/reports on accepted CV program success metrics; evidence of significant portfolio wins and parent/external approbation
The Challenge	How to design, test and operate at speed while most vulnerable to natural corporate antibodies and external ecosystem skepticism	How to demonstrate CV program strategic relevance and make case for expansion while retaining and growing high-performance specialist team	How to stay relevant, agile through environmental oscillations without damaging CV program brand or disenfranchising portfolio and partners

High Performer Programs/Teams to Lead the Way

Chapters 3–5 set out "Design Rules" for programs at each stage of development across the five operational dimensions. At the end of each chapter are illustrative "high-performer" profiles for leading programs at each stage of development, as learning from others who have "been there and done that" is often the best, most compelling path to progress. Profiles include:

- Start-up phase: Capital One Growth Ventures, CSAA SI, JetBlue Technology Ventures
- Expansion phase: Echo Health Ventures, Munich Re Ventures
- Resiliency Phase: Citi Ventures, Intel Capital, Merck Global Health Innovation Fund

---

These leading programs represent a range of sectors, CV models, and approaches and maturity levels—and all line up around Fifth Wave core principles and have these characteristics in common:

- Experienced CV&I leader, and a team that blends professionals from outside and inside the company, including senior dedicated investment (CVC) and corporate venture business development (CVBD) professionals.
- A sophisticated and informed program plan and charter driven by an initial, directional vision and big ideas. Embodies end-to-end investing principles that are the hallmark of corporate venturing— from idea and sourcing through to executable landing spots of commercial and strategic benefit to parent.
- Significant program and performance acceleration ("leap frogging"—platform-building, rapid portfolio development, and program/fund expansion in a fraction of time of predecessors).
- Consistency of C-level champions; respected program/practitioner position within the company and within the external innovation investment ecosystem.
- Excellence in venture board and observer roles, with purposefully trained and seasoned CV team members who can optimize the balance between parent risks and venture value creation. Respected by and sought after by co-investors and venture teams.
- CV&I leader has a "seat at the table:" now an integral part of a team of high-level execs who set the business priorities and strategy that sets the course for the future of the parent.

CHAPTER 3

Start-Up Phase (Years 0–3)

The **Goal:** Earn parent and external respect by accelerating early indicators of being "on track" with a savvy, professional CV program. ("No dabbling")

What's Happening:

- **Focus**: Accelerate foundational design and first build-out of the CV program "platform"—charter, core team, governance, operations, ecosystems
- **Operating style**: Testing while doing—build, test, refine, operationalize
- **Performance**: Start the clock for speed of program development, quality, and path to performance

The Challenge: *How to design, test, and operate at speed while most vulnerable to natural corporate antibodies and external ecosystem skepticism.*

Executive Summary

With the growth and mainstreaming of corporate venturing as a fundamental corporate innovation tool, CV programs are playing more active roles in corporate strategy development, including advising established businesses, exploring adjacencies and new business models, and providing insights on future trends and technologies.

However, with increasing executive willingness to invest hundreds of millions in new CV programs comes the expectation that those programs be able to demonstrate both early traction and strategic impact, typically within a twenty-four-to-thirty-six-month "corporate patience cycle."

To that end, new entrants, often led by experienced CV professionals, are applying lessons learned from industry predecessors to set new high bars for program acceleration and quality.

High-Performer Hallmarks

1. **Program vision** for impact drives clear charter and operating model
2. **Seasoned team** blends internal and VC ecosystem operating experience
3. Proactive expectation setting for **CV program performance and milestones**

Accelerated teams start with a set of innovation investment opportunity hypotheses, and a guiding vision for how to both maximize the value of those investments and make them most impactful for the parent. Capturing foundational assumptions about goals, investment strategy, and operating model in a concise charter helps to promote clarity and facilitates executive commitment to the program.

At this point, supporting CV program structure, people, and process are honed for internal/external agility and adaptability: less is more (the Minimum Viable Program).

The team—which may include internal, external, and specialist outsourced resources—blends CV and market/ecosystem domain expertise with the ability to effectively navigate the parent. It's a harder job than venture capital investing.

At this vulnerable stage of program development, the CV team takes the lead in iterative performance expectation setting—translating CV program development and performance management experience into context, interim milestones and KPIs expressed in language that is meaningful to the parent. Early strategic communications highlight evidence of program quality, team CV expertise, and ability to earn respect, both internally and externally.

Threats and Antibodies

But, like developing a start-up business, new CV program creation is hard. It requires live testing while rapidly building the program "platform" (charter, professional team, operations and governance structures, ecosystems), and at the same time constantly ducking and weaving around the natural corporate antibodies that arise to attack new and foreign activities.

Early friction points:

- **The "time sink"**—educating and engaging the parent

  For the CV program leader, it may be close to a full-time job to obtain and retain both parent executive management and business operational support for an activity that is seldom well understood on the inside but must appear credible and professional on the outside. This won't change—plan for it.

- **Exception-based recruiting**—rationalization for new CV role creation

  The senior levels/titles and specialty compensation packages required to compete for experienced CV teams typically fall outside the traditional corporate HR structures and practices, necessitating exception-based recruiting. Not sustainable at scale.

- **The "maturation gap"**—internal/external positioning

  It's always a challenge to balance internal (professional CV team, compelling vision, early traction, and value delivery) and external (committed/credible investor, value-adding partner with ecosystem vision) positioning and perceptions as there is often a "maturation gap" that the CV team must finesse in the early stages of CV program development. Key message: no "dabbling."

Start-Up Phase Design Rules
Charter

1. **Define foundational CV program vision for impactful end-to-end investing** (from sourcing through landing spots)

   Accelerated CV program teams and corporate parents have ongoing clarifying conversations to tune strategic investment goals to leverage parent competencies/market leadership and respond to business urgencies. And at the same time, they envision roadmaps for developing the innovation partnerships, blended CV team/capabilities, and operating models needed to maximize the future impact of strategic investments.

Citi Ventures from the beginning envisioned an approach and CV team structure designed to drive maximum value both from investments and from strategic engagement with innovative teams both inside and outside Citi.

"We have formed a unique, foundational team of CV investment and business development/partnering specialists to deliver on our charter... to invest in start-ups to transform the future of financial services and enhance Citi's position in determining that course."
(Source: Citi Ventures website)

---

2. **Make CV program charter explicit and get management commitment**

   A program charter represents a rallying document outlining CV program strategy and investment approach: objectives, focus areas, investment models, approach, and melding of financial and strategic performance goals. (See Sample CVC Program Charter Outline box.)

   Particularly for corporations that are new to corporate venturing, charter discussions can be invaluable in establishing common ground on program investment objectives/goals as well as educating investment committee members and executives on venture capital investing.

Sample CVC Program Charter Outline

Investment Objectives	• Develop transformation opportunities for parent • Gain unique, asymmetric view into emerging tech areas • ID key talent, networks, tech, and business models for acquisition, licensing, or partnership • Achieve ~ 3X return on invested capital across portfolio
Investment Focus	• Technology and businesses related to parent businesses • Target (list of strategic focus areas)
Investment Models/ Types	• Generally direct minority investments in private companies • Prioritize Series A–C • Select investments in VC funds with unique strategies or focus on geographic regions or early stage (pre-seed, seed) investments
Investment Structure	• Preferred stock, convertible debt • Less than 20% of voting stock in C-Corp, less than 5% of LLCs or partnerships
Investment Geography	• Globally but generally North America
Investment Amounts	• $1–10M for typical investments plus follow-ons • Larger amounts if PE/structured buyouts
Syndication	• Deal dependent on other VCs or investment groups as lead or co-lead
Holding Period	• 5–7 years
Portfolio Size	• 15–20 investments across 10-year LRP
Exit Strategy	• Acquisition by 3rd parties, IPO, Parent M&A, liquidation

3. **Design for longevity and impact**—CV program reporting, structure, funding

As critical evidence of corporate commitment to the CV program, recent years have seen consistent "up-leveling" of reporting for air cover...with CEO as active supporter and program lead no more than two layers down.

Furthermore, CV program reporting has shifted to the business commercial/transactional side—corporate strategy, business development, corporate development. Even those with strong technology/ digital transformation charter reporting through R&D often have matrixed commercial executive management performance oversight.

Other indicators of corporate willingness to formalize CV as a critical innovation tool:

- Legal structure: More common use of external vehicles such as LLCs to simplify internal corporate financial reporting and provide downstream vehicle for CV program expansion and specialist team retention.

- Funding: Corporate multiyear CV program commitments to support active investing/follow-ons (5+/year, team of 5-6 can ramp to 10+). Typical first fund equals $100–$150 million.

- Portfolio development: Emerging use of what Ron Arnold of IAG Firemark Ventures calls "leverage funds" or designated budgets to facilitate parent/portfolio collaborations (trials, pilots, etc.)

Process

4. **Align CV governance with competitive VC investing expectations**

The role of CV governance is to represent/promote the strategic interests of the corporation, evaluate the quality of deals, and assess potential risks. An effective CV investment committee is small, educated on VC investing, and committed to being informed, agile, and predictable. (See Sample Investment Committee Structure and Charter box.)

A larger population of interested parties/internal stakeholders may participate formally or informally through the investment diligence process, advisory councils, innovation networks, and ongoing CV team outreach.

Sample Investment Committee Structure and Charter

Investment Committee Make-Up	• 5–7 members (subsection of Executive Team) • CEO, CFO, CTO, CSO, relevant BU head(s) • Risk Review Board as needed for compliance
Key Objectives	• Validate strategic direction relative to corporate priorities; facilitate landing spots • Review current investment portfolio • Review investment strategy, priorities, portfolio creation • Approve –Final term sheet submissions –Investments and follow-ons –Seed investments –Liquidations, sales of companies
Responsibilities	• Be up to date on current investment portfolio • Assist in driving strategic value from portfolio via expertise and network connections • Read and understand term sheets, cap tables • Support institutionalization of CV program (for efficiency, continuity, internal and external reputation enhancement)
Mechanics	• Frequency: –IC meets every 6 weeks plus ad hoc as needed –Weekly deal-flow update materials provided • Materials: PowerPoint (low artistry) and Excel • Meeting format: Telecons and in person

5. **Develop agile CV-specific deal management/investing process**

Seasoned CV teams come with an understanding of how to balance competitive VC deal timeframes with just enough diligence, rigor, and standardized deal structuring. (See Mark Radcliffe/DLA Piper Q&A on CVC financing and legal considerations.) Ideally the team has the autonomy to develop a streamlined independent investment process. Corporations seeking to use existing product development or M&A processes/systems to manage CV deals often find that it's much harder and more time-consuming to make a $1 million investment than a $100 million acquisition.

Increased corporate openness to more agile/lean CV invest-ment and partnering decision-making processes reflects greater parent understanding of the specialized nature of the CV practice and experience of the team. In some cases, this comes with higher levels of signatory authority than in the past, sometimes as high as $1 million.

Q&A with Mark Radcliffe/DLA Piper: What are the critical financing and legal considerations for corporations establishing corporate venture capital investing processes?

Mark Radcliffe: The major characteristics of the venture capital ecosystem (including the corporate venture capital components) have changed over the last thirty years, but certain fundamentals have remained the same: (1) Financing structures continue to use preferred stock for investors (and common stock and common stock options, respectively, for founders and employees), and the terms have become more standardized in the last ten years, but in the last five years, terms at very early stage and very late stage (financing for "unicorns") have become less standardized–understanding those terms and the acceptable modifications are critical to success for CVC investors; and (2) venture capital transactions continue to be a "specialist legal practice," and corporate venture capital is even more specialized since its issues differ from traditional financial venture capital.

Financing Terms: Most start-ups understand that growth will require a series of financings, and investors will expect financing terms which are "industry standard." During my thirty years of practice, the terms of venture capital financing transactions have become more standard, with the rise of standard forms such as Series Seed, SAFE, and National Venture Capital Association (NVCA).

However, these forms are designed for traditional financial investors, and corporate venture capitalists should recognize that they may need different terms because of their internal needs and regulatory requirements.

For example, the confidentiality provisions of the traditional NVCA are too restrictive for many corporate venture capitalists who need to share information from their investments with their finance departments. One particularly sensitive area is the degree of control or notice in the case of a potential merger exit. More than 90 percent of start-ups exit by a merger. The venture capital operations of some corporations are concerned about the potential sale of the start-up to a competing company. Yet start-up and traditional financial venture capital investors will want to ensure that the start-up has the greatest possible flexibility in seeking a merger partner. Some corporations believe that an investment by the corporation is so important that they can demand a "right of first refusal" for any sale of start-up, but these terms *will not be acceptable* to virtually all start-ups (and their traditional financial investors).

In addition, corporate venture capital investors may be subject to regulatory regimes, such as the Bank Secrecy Act, that do not apply to traditional financial venture capitalists. These regimes may require special terms, and corporate venture capitalists should be prepared have a standard approach that can be explained to the start-up in which they intend to invest.

Legal Considerations: The basic legal framework for venture capital financing transactions has remained the same during my thirty-five years of practice: investors receive preferred stock, founders receive common stock, and employees receive options to purchase common stock. And start-ups raise money in a series of preferred stock financings.

Although the basic legal deal framework remains the same, the implementation of these terms is critical to the success of a start-up (and its investors). The failure to use the traditional framework can make a new round of preferred stock funding more difficult or even impossible. However, the last five years have seen important new issues arise: new terms, such as guaranteed returns, in late-stage fundings for "unicorns" (private companies with a valuation of $1 billion which did exist prior to 2014) and the rise of initial coin offerings as alternative to traditional venture capital.

We are seeing the rise of new structures in corporate venture organizations, such as separate "internal" funds for different entities within the parent company and separate funds including only corporate investors. In addition, these transactions require that outside counsel work closely with in-house counsel (who rarely have experience with this type of transaction) and who will seek outside counsel with significant corporate venture capital experience. Consequently, the selection of experienced counsel is important for both internal and external reasons.

6. **Plan for development and integration of CV business development (CVBD) function**

　　With early investments, the CV team learns from experience about how best to deliver on the end-to-end investing vision and plan for expansion. Where are the best parent champions and middle management touchpoints (for strategy input and operational engagement)? Who is best suited to take on, and project manage parent-portfolio engagements? How to ensure that the value of those engagements is captured? Should CVBD resources be matrixed, rotating, or sourced externally?

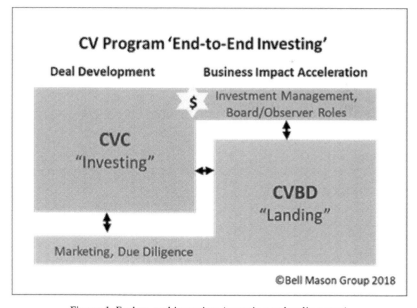

Figure 1: End-to-end investing (sourcing to landing spot)

Team

7. **Tap visionary CV program leader with ability to recruit high performers, evangelize internally, and impress externally**

    Like the CEO/founder of a start-up, the accelerated CV program leader needs to bring the vision and expertise to be credible and able to engage potential recruits, activate a powerful internal network, and convince the external ecosystem of the potential value and quality of a nascent program. Best positioning for the role is no more than two levels below the CEO, with a title at VP level or above. (See Sample CV Program Leader job description box.)

CV Program Leader—Senior Corporate Executive (VP level or above) Plans/manages entire CV operation and organization. Senior executive leader responsible for innovation investment portfolio strategy and development, reporting, and unit/program performance. Key responsibilities:

- Interface with executive leadership of parent company (e.g. CEO, CFO, COO, CTO, CDO, CSO); responsible for board reporting
- Maintain connections to corporate leadership at business unit and functional level
- Participate in parent cross-corporate councils and task forces and provide strategic advice
- Be external "face" of CV program—build/manage external investing and corporate ecosystem partner networks, serve as key spokesperson (conferences, parent events, press, etc.)
- Serve as board/observer rep for key portfolio companies' board meetings
- Recruit and manage high-performance team

Experience: Typically has ten to fifteen years of experience or more in CVC/VC/banking with a track record in deal making, partnering, corporate development, and/or business development roles. Holds

---

advanced business degree and may have relevant technology/scientific education.

Largest individual compensation package and bonus.

8. **Hire CV expertise and experience (fit person to job, not job to person)**—Go outside when not available inside

Increasingly CV program teams are pairing senior internal people fluent in parent language, culture, and business with senior specialist outsiders who bring CVC/VC/PE/I-Bank or start-up company experience. Thelander CV compensation research shows that on average, more than 50 percent of CV teams come from the outside. Corporates new to corporate venturing are showing respect for experienced CV professionals recruited to fill parent capability gaps and accelerate quality program development...and who understand the unique challenges of the multisided CV (versus VC) model.

Particularly in these early days, the team needs to be comfortable functioning with uncertainty, and demonstrating "plasticity," operating agility, and adaptability, which are critical for program survival.

Also critical is permission to look externally for key CV specialist competencies not available internally (e.g., legal, tax and accounting, compensation, deal data, search, innovation strategy, and landscaping).

For example, CV teams can get up and running quickly and effectively by adopting a legal team construct that combines experienced venture capital outside counsel and in-house counsel (who are unlikely to be experienced with such "specialized" transactions). In-house counsel is critical to the success of CVC units but are not likely to have the time to become deeply familiar with such transactions, and experienced outside counsel can assist in ensuring that the CVC unit maintains its reputation as a sophisticated member of the venture capital ecosystem.

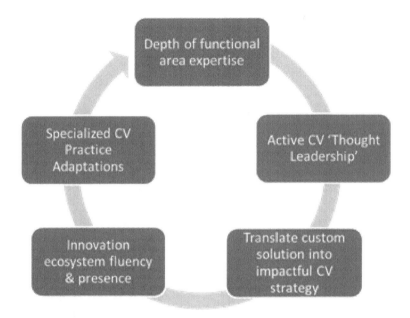

Figure 2: Characteristics of high-quality CV service providers

9. **Develop roadmap for CV team recruitment and retention** (compensation and career paths)

    With the explosive growth of new CV programs has come the need to compete to recruit (and retain) experienced CVC investment and business development professionals from a highly competitive investment ecosystem talent pool drawn from other CVCs, VCs, PE firms, I-Banks, and private companies. Through research and a data platform pioneered by J. Thelander Consulting, broad investment ecosystem and vertical sector compensation package benchmarks are now available for increasingly CV-standardized roles. (See Corporate Venture Program Roles Tracked in Annual Thelander Compensation Research box.)

    Corporate willingness to recruit top talent with exception-based packages and to evolve HR structures, compensation packages, titling, and career paths will be a test of ongoing commitment to the program.

Corporate Venture Program Roles Tracked in Annual Thelander Compensation Research

- CV unit leader, senior corporate level executive
- Senior investment professional
- Dedicated CV in-house counsel
- CV unit portfolio manager/CFO
- Portfolio development/corporate venture business development (CVBD) leader
- Portfolio development/corporate venture business development professional
- Investment/program manager
- Associate/analyst

Thelander data can be used to normalize compensation benchmarks across the Investment Firm ecosystem. While corporate venture and venture capital firms share the same talent pool, the compensation structures and risk/reward profiles are different. While VCs may have a higher potential upside over time in the form of "carried interest," they also must contribute capital and fundraise and be prepared to wait for an uncertain reward.

Competitive CVC packages may include competitive base salaries with more certain bonuses, including a combination of cash and RSUs in the parent company. There are variations on these models, and understanding the nuances is the Thelander expertise. Covering over 850 investment firms annually, Thelander provides both data and in-depth analysis across the VC, CVC, and private company universe.

Innovation Partnering

10. **Internal ecosystem: Establish active top-level sponsorship and define strategy for operational engagement with middle management**

    As key success factors for delivering value to both corporate parent and external partners, a recent survey of Health Evolution

Summit Corporate Venture Group (HE-CVG) members highlighted the importance of combining top-level CV program sponsorships

---

Hewlett Packard Ventures–Parent Engagement Starts at the Top

For a young Hewlett Packard Ventures, the top success factor for accelerated CV program visibility and effectiveness was a CEO who understood entrepreneurship and saw start-up relationships as a critical component of corporate growth and innovation strategy. HPE CEO Meg Whitman set the parent tone by highlighting the Ventures/Pathfinder program with main-stage visibility at flagship customer marketing events, conducting quarterly "coffee talks" with portfolio companies/prospects (attendance mandatory for her direct reports), and removing roadblocks to engagement opportunities.

For Hewlett Packard Ventures, engagement meant incorporating a start-up's offer into a solution for HPE customers, so Pathfinder Academy was established for the enablement and training of key customer account managers (including meetings with CV portfolio companies). And HPE Complete, a process for getting third-party solutions onto the price list with sales incentives and sympathetic partnership terms, was put in place.

---

with programs for addressing the "soft middle" of the corporation to drive operational parent-portfolio engagement.

11. **External ecosystem: Prioritize investment strategic focus areas and develop target external ecosystem maps**

CSAA Insurance Group's young S&I team started by developing focused Point of View (POV) white papers to explore key trends, reimagine parent product/service opportunities, and map innovation/venture landscapes to guide make/buy/partner/invest decisions.

Establish a process and model for developing, describing, and refining strategic focus areas to guide external network outreach and targeted presence, and to improve quality of the innovation opportunity pipeline.

12. **Articulate and validate CV program quality and value to portfolio companies and syndicate partners (transparency, predictable process, value)**

    As corporates have broadly acknowledged CV as a mainstream innovation tool, institutional investors and other players/stakeholders in the innovation-investment ecosystem are recognizing the significant value that professionally managed CV programs can deliver with powerful parent brands, channels and domain expertise. However, BMG research has shown that investment program credibility is dependent on the ability to deliver that value with clear investment strategies, predictable CV operating processes, well-established internal corporate networks, and CV team expertise in facilitating impactful relationships between start-ups and corporate parents. (See Innovation Partner-Readiness Checklist at end of chapter 3 Design Rules.)

Performance

13. **Define directional CV program development timeline with incremental milestones and measures**

    Indicate what's possible in the start-up years (when the program is most embryonic and vulnerable), often "flying under the radar" internally. The goal is to earn early respect for a specialized CV practice and professionals.

14. **Test and document CV program ability to deliver appropriate strategic-financial value mix**

    Strive for increasing clarity and concreteness in CV program charters that fuse strategic goals (commercial traction, other impact goals) with financial performance targets (don't lose money, institutional VC partner returns metrics).

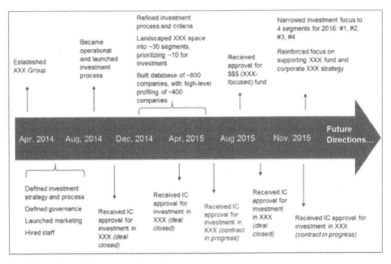

Figure 3: Sample program start-up timeline

Hewlett Packard Ventures–Early Proof of Program Value

The Hewlett Packard Ventures team hit the ground running. In April of Year 1, Hewlett Packard Enterprise selected Sequoia-backed Israeli start-up Adallom to enhance their offerings with a cloud application security layer and made a minority investment through their Hewlett Packard Ventures Unit. Six months later Adallom was acquired by Microsoft, netting a nice financial return on the investment to complement the strategic value derived through the advanced technology/distribution relationship.

Look for early evidence, and through experience, iteratively define, quantify, and track what matters to the parent and monitor how long it takes to get there. Be realistic about the overhead required to collect and report on performance data.

15. **Define communications strategy and plan**

At this vulnerable stage of program development, a proactive CV team takes the lead in iterative performance expectation setting—translating CV program development and performance management experience into context, interim milestones, and KPIs expressed in language that is meaningful to the parent. Early strategic communications highlight evidence of program quality, team CV expertise, and ability to earn respect, both internally and externally.

In the early days, limit the scope of communication activity to continue to fly under the radar, given the state of development and the challenge of inward lack of preparedness versus outside "market face." It's risky to get further ahead externally of where you are internally, with potential for damaging corporate and program reputation until the "struts" are better in place.

CV Program: Innovation Partner-Readiness Checklist

CV Innovation Partner-Readiness Priorities	Examples
Clear investment strategy (Including unified front with other parent innovation programs)	• Defined charter, investment strategy, and program performance metrics • Unified corporate face to outside (key domains, open innovation activities) • Comes to start-up and investor meetings prepared and ready to "give to get" as a good ecosystem partner
Predictable, streamlined CV operating processes (Understand VC and start-up game)	• Dedicated CV specialist team, investment funds • "Competitive" process for deal management (DD, term sheet negotiation, valuation, governance, close, funds transfer, etc.) • Funds earmarked for follow-on investments • Capable, experienced board members/observers who understand venture development and that their duty is to venture first, parent second (avoiding conflicts of interest)
Well-established internal corporate networks	• Corporate leadership access and champions (2 below CEO) • Influence at right levels in key internal units • Cross-company domain expertise and connections
Expertise in facilitating value-adding venture–corporate parent relationships	• Ability to access/deliver corporate, domain expertise and resources in a timely manner • Prepared to advise on, monitor, and troubleshoot parent commercial business-start-up relationship issues

Start-Up Phase Design Rules

Charter	1. Define foundational CV program vision for impactful end-to-end investing 2. Make CV program charter explicit and get management commitment 3. Design for longevity and impact
Process	4. Align CV governance with competitive VC investing expectations 5. Develop agile CV-specific deal management/ investing process 6. Plan for development and integration of CV business development (CVBD) function
Team	7. Tap visionary CV program leader with ability to recruit high performers, evangelize internally, and impress externally 8. Hire CV expertise and experience 9. Develop CV team recruitment/retention roadmap
Innovation Partnering	10. Internal Ecosystem: Establish active top-level sponsorship and define strategy for operational engagement with middle management 11. External ecosystem: Prioritize investment strategic focus areas and develop target external ecosystem maps 12. Articulate and validate CV program quality and value to portfolio companies and syndicate partners
Performance	13. Define directional CV program development timeline with incremental milestones and measures 14. Test and document CV program ability to deliver appropriate strategic-financial value mix 15. Define communications strategy and plan

HIGH PERFORMER PROFILES
Start-Up Phase (Years 0–3)
PROGRAM PROFILE: CAPITAL ONE GROWTH VENTURES

Program Name	Capital One Growth Ventures (COGV)
Date Established	2015
Parent HQ and CV Locations	Capital One: McLean, VA (USA) Capital One Growth Ventures: San Francisco; New York; McLean, VA; Washington, DC
Charter	Working alongside passionate entrepreneurs, COGV's goal is to help start-ups gain traction, evolve, and deliver disruptive new technologies and solutions that drive major innovation for Capital One's businesses and breakthrough experiences for Capital One's customers. • Near term (0–6 months): Meet current Capital One needs and opportunities • Medium term (6–18 months): Achieve, accelerate, or enhance Capital One's roadmap and strategic goals • Long term (18–30 months): Influence direction of Capital One's markets and businesses
Legal, Reporting Structure	• Capital One business group and investment company subsidiary • Reports to chief enterprise services officer
CV Program Elements	• Venture investing (CVC) • Venture development (corporate venture business development) • Community management
Team Size	• Venture investing (8) • Venture development (2) • Community management (2)
Focus Areas	• Data and tech infrastructure • Enterprise SaaS • Security and authentication • Payments, fintech, and consumer

Program Scale	• 21 active venture portfolio companies; exited Paydiant (PayPal), Chain (Interstellar) • Executed 3 minority investments for LOBs • Sourced 2 corporate acquisitions • Annual run rate: 6–8 investments
Recent Sample Investments	• Enigma • Dave • Verodin • ThoughtSpot • Snowflake (multiple rounds)
Select Syndicate Partners	• VC: Sutter Hill, Khosla Ventures, Redpoint Ventures, Menlo Ventures, Felicis Ventures, Madrona Ventures, Point72 Ventures • CVC: Citi Ventures • Other: Altimeter Capital Management

Description of Program Development Journey and Key Learnings

To shape and lead a new corporate venturing initiative, Capital One tapped Jaidev Shergill, a veteran financial services and CVC executive, as well as the CEO of a start-up recently acquired by Capital One. Shergill's charter and operating vision for Capital One Growth Ventures (COGV) was to match attractive start-ups' disruptive technologies and business models with opportunities to address the challenges and needs of Capital One's businesses and customers.

From the start, Shergill envisioned an end-to-end investing approach (source-invest-partner-land-expand) powered by a high-performance COGV platform and team.

In the first phase of planning and development, COGV focused on designing and building out the CVC process to make and manage good investments and ensure the portfolio was connected to Capital One.

The second phase, currently underway, is about learning from early experience and formalizing what COGV calls the Venture Development function. Venture Development includes the delivery of programs and a team of professionals responsible for identifying and managing landing spots for portfolio companies within Capital One. Having learned through iterative experiences that internal introductions are only a starting point in the journey to lasting impact, this specialized venture development capability is critical to the CV program's ability to maximize the strategic value of start-up investments to Capital One.

The COGV Investment and Venture Development teams and processes are designed to be highly synergistic, collaborative, and integrated to make good on this ambidextrous program approach.

This approach is proving to be a win-win for both Capital One and COGV's portfolio companies. COGV's early track record is turning initial "push" (creating demand internally) into "pull" (demand comes to you):

- Capital One businesses now share their requirements and problems with COGV and ask for insight on tech/market trends and existing portfolio company capabilities. This engagement creates opportunities to collaborate early on new products and roadmaps, increasing the potential to develop strategically valuable relationships.

■ Start-ups want to have robust product pipelines and see the value of Capital One as both a contributor to their product/business roadmaps and a key reference customer.

Key COGV Program Design Elements

1. **Vision for end-to-end investing**

   COGV's team structure and collaborative processes are designed and continuously honed to support portfolio companies through each part of the lifecycle, from funding to testing in the real world to rapid growth.

   The specialist Investment team is divided between the technology and financial services centers of San Francisco and New York. The Venture Development team, combining a senior internal resource and an external specialist (with experience from In-Q-Tel's best-in-class tech partnering program), is local to Capital One just outside of Washington, DC.

   Both teams collaborate in an overlapping, end-to-end process, starting with the Venture Development team having a vote in the deal evaluation process and the Investment team managing post investment relationships with portfolio companies.

   Over the last three years, the COGV team built a well-performing portfolio with first-tier syndicate partners. COGV is showing both good financial returns on its on-balance sheet capital and clear strategic benefits from both deployments and market insights.

2. **Understanding of Capital One culture and how it works**

   Before engaging with start-ups and starting investment discussions, new COGV team hires are all expected to spend significant time with the businesses and functions to build relationships and understand internal perspectives and points of leverage.

This understanding is fundamental to making the CV program a "must-have" platform for the organization. The team asks: What are the big boulders COGV can help move for Capital One? The problem needs to be big enough—"beyond noise"—and the points of leverage must be clear.

Also, COGV recognizes the value of its parent's business accomplishments to date, and the depth of learnings and perspective it has garnered in the process. For example, three years ago many venture firms were eager to invest in alternative lenders. Capital One lending experts provided great historical perspective on credit, lending, and compliance operations, as well as the potential for significant downside. This perspective persuaded COGV not to invest in this sector and to avoid potential losses.

3. **Focus on repeatable process—Venture Operations Playbook**

From day one, the COGV team formalized and documented all of its processes in a Venture Operations Playbook. Periodically refined and updated, the playbook drives repeatability at predictable quality and is essential to program scalability. The team learned to work through the unique challenges that come with operating in a regulated industry (e.g., time needed for legal, compliance, regulatory, and finance approvals) as well as the added consideration of ensuring investment committee decisions can be made within the typical venture financing timeline. COGV devised a unique internal due diligence process that identifies early on the potential for downstream challenges in getting an investment approved. This enables the team to provide early insight, process transparency and clarity on potential issues to prospective ventures.

The quality of the deal as a financial investment and the potential strategic value to Capital One drive investment decision-making. Both the Investment Partner (financial focus) and the Venture Development Partner (strategic value focus) need to agree for a deal to move forward. After making an investment, the Growth Ventures team and Capital One business partners agree and track ongoing success metrics.

Best Example of How Business Model Works: ThoughtSpot

Strategic rationale: While there was no immediate use case at the time of investment, Capital One was drawn to ThoughtSpot's product roadmap and long-term vision, coupled with its unique approach to data and business intelligence.

Strategic value realized: In the first year after investment, one Capital One business conducted a successful proof of concept with limited scope. After continued development of the ThoughtSpot platform, along with meetings and demos across Capital One, ThoughtSpot signed a commercial agreement with Capital One's tech group.

Mutual benefits: ThoughtSpot provided value around new approaches to data discovery and BI. ThoughtSpot's product leadership consulted with Capital One teams. Capital One in turn provided ThoughtSpot with strategic input that helped lead to broader commercial adoption.

Perspective: Top Three Things Deemed Essential to COGV Program Development and Scale

1. **Retention of high performing investment and venture development professionals**

    Capital One Growth Ventures is making progress in establishing the group as a leading investor in the enterprise tech, data, cybersecurity and fintech markets, and in building the relationships necessary to gain access to quality deals and land them within Capital One.

    COGV has been successful in attracting high-performing investments and venture development talent in a highly competitive market. The ability to retain these and other core specialists will depend on 1) COGV offering market-competitive CV compensation packages with rewards and incentive structures unique to Capital One, and 2) creating COGV-specific career paths.

2. **Active COGV role in Capital One technology innovation and business strategy development**

COGV team works to keep Capital One business and functional partners collaboratively engaged by regularly discussing and helping set their strategic innovation goals. For example, the business or function will frame their strategy, needs, and technology architecture in key areas; COGV will then commit to bringing relevant start-ups in these areas on a consistent basis.

3. **COGV proactive approach to measuring performance and strategy for program growth**

According to Shergill, "The first 2 years is the honeymoon phase; year 3 must show results."

The COGV team is advancing to the next phase of growth essential for maintaining pace and position in the market as well as delivering increasing impact to Capital One. In its early phase, COGV quickly built out and validated its vision-driven plan, program fundamentals, core team, and platform. It made high-quality investments and drove strategic venture development that ensured Capital One landing spots for most of the portfolio. The team is now focused on extending and building on their initial success to ensure they consistently evolve and deliver on strategy, serving as a meaningful and core contributor to Capital One's broader corporate strategy.

The going forward plan contains three main elements:

1. Increased venture development staff to develop deeper understanding of and partnership with Capital One's business and tech groups.
2. Expanded deliverables to generate strategic value beyond investments and commercial adoption.
3. Test capabilities and infrastructure to evaluate new technology and products more rapidly, and to accelerate time to strategic value.

How Is COGV Measured?

Capital One being a historically data-driven company, GOGV focuses on quantitative decision-making and reporting. COGV designed and formalized an evaluation and portfolio performance tracking system that measures both strategic value realized and financial performance at both portfolio and CV partner levels.

Start-up companies are scored on both strategic and financial dimensions before going to the investment committee. Semiannually, COGV updates strategic value scores and analyzes financial performance for each portfolio company.

1. **Strategic potential**
    - Scored in advance of investment, then semiannually
    - Eight weighted variables for areas including investor relationship value, vendor relationship impact, and learning and culture impact

Figure 4: Capital One Growth Ventures Strategic Value Scoring

2. Financial success probability

- Scored in advance of investment
- Eighteen weighted variables for areas including management and investors, product innovation, unit economics, macro conditions, and price versus performance

COGV is expanding and adapting this system for use in assessing and tracking potential co-investors and partners for their complementary strategic capabilities, development support, and financial prowess. This is the foundation of the next level of quantitative measurement: a portfolio partner evaluation and tracking system, essentially for "curating" the most attractive co-investors and strategic partners for COGV's and Capital One's priorities.

PROGRAM PROFILE: CSAA INSURANCE GROUP, STRATEGY & INNOVATION

Program Name	CSAA Insurance Group, Strategy & Innovation (CSAA business unit)
Date Established	November 2016
HQ & Locations	Parent: San Francisco Bay Area (Walnut Creek, CA) Strategy & Innovation: CSAA IG HQ; CVC office in Mountain View, CA
Charter	The Strategy & Innovation team's mission is to "innovate our future" by creating new products, services, and ventures that deliver extraordinary value to current and future AAA members. We are aiming high with an audacious goal to create $1 billion in new revenue in the next decade. Toward this end, we are building a portfolio of growth initiatives through a combination of new business incubation, commercial piloting, venture investing, strategic partnerships, and business development. The result will be new sources of value and relevance to current and future AAA members, expansion and diversification of our business, and competitive advantage in the markets we serve.
Legal Structure	• CSAA Business unit, led by chief strategy & innovation officer • Reports to CEO
CV Program elements	• Corporate Strategy & Partnerships (development/ ownership) • CVC (+ LP in automotive seed fund; M&A channel) • Innovation–core/sustaining/disruptive • Labs–prototyping, proofs-of-concept (POCs)

Team Size (25)	• Chief Strategy & Innovation Officer Debbie Brackeen (externally recruited) • Strategy & partnerships: 6, led by VP (internally recruited) • CVC: 6, led by managing partner (externally recruited) • Innovation: 7, led by VP (internally recruited) • Labs: 4, led by interim head (internal) • Administrative staff: 1
Focus Areas	• InsurTech • Mobility, connected car, autonomous vehicles • IoT & connected home • Analytics & AI/machine learning • Blockchain applications
Program Scale	• Innovation pipeline: 14 active projects • CVC portfolio: 3 portfolio companies; 3 LP investments • CVC average investments: 3–5/year, Series A/Series B, off balance sheet
Recent Sample Investments	• Owl Cameras (intelligent LTE vehicle security camera) • Cape Analytics (satellite/aerial imagery + AI to assess property condition) • Rapid SOS (links any connected device to 911 and first responders)
Sample Syndicate Partners	• VC: Menlo Ventures, Khosla Ventures, Playground Ventures, Highland Capital, Sherpa Capital, Canvas Ventures, Data Collective, Forte Ventures • CVC: Microsoft Ventures, Motorola Ventures, Hartford Ventures, XL Innovate • Other: TechStars

Description of Program Development Journey and Key Learnings

CSAA Insurance Group is a $4 billion company that provides personal auto, home, and other insurance products to AAA members exclusively through its AAA club partners in twenty-three states and Washington, DC.

Recognizing significant near- and long-term threats to its core business and competitive position, seven years ago CSAA IG committed to a major transformation of its business in order to position the company to compete effectively in the future. Specific objectives included:

- Modernizing products
- Updating technology platform to systems that are modern and scalable
- Expanding digital capabilities
- Deploying an industry-leading data and analytics platform and a new CRM tool
- Transforming its corporate culture to be more innovative and agile

The first step was an overhaul of CSAA's IT infrastructure (responding to on-demand, digital, mobile requirements) to create a new foundation for improved operating efficiency, security, data analytics, and customer service related to present products/services as well those that could drive its future.

The second was to commit significant investment and mindshare to accelerating new CSAA business creation through innovation. The chief strategy and innovation officer role (member of CSAA Executive Management Team) was created and filled in 2016 by Debbie Brackeen, a seasoned venturing and innovation senior executive with a long track record of leadership success in Silicon Valley building programs at Apple, e-Bay, VC-backed start-ups, HP, and Citi Group.

With CEO Paula Downey as champion, Brackeen was tasked with developing a large scale, first-of-kind CSAA innovation program focused on generating $1 billion in new revenue within a decade. Recognizing that the $1 billion bogey requires a mix of organic and inorganic growth, Brackeen envisioned a mix of corporate venturing and innovation (CV&I) program elements, team structures, end-to-end investment processes, and culture change initiatives designed to create and land a pipeline of "outside-in and inside-out" innovation and significant new business/revenue generation opportunities for CSAA.

Key CSAA S&I Program Design Elements

1. **Mandate—Innovation positioned as core tenet of CSAA corporate strategy**

   Brackeen's combined strategy and innovation role and seat on the CSAA Executive Leadership Team reinforce the importance of innovation in fulfilling CSAA IG's dual strategic imperatives to optimize and grow the core, and to place strategic bets for future growth and diversification. Integration of the two functions highlights the goal of making innovation a CSAA core competency, strategic differentiator, and revenue generator.

2. **Organization structure—Corporate innovation engine structure and operating processes**

   The S&I organization combines all the major innovation functions in a single organization, allowing for leveraging insights and capturing synergies across all—strategy, partnerships, innovation, labs, CVC, and M&A. Some teams are co-located with and closely aligned to the core business; other teams are free to operate separate from the core leveraging shared work spaces like Galvanize and soon-to-open Silicon Valley office. The outside-in/inside-out programs allow teams to quickly bridge between external innovation/ecosystems and internal CSAA core businesses and functions.

   After the second full year, the foundation is in place, and programs are delivering early proof points and validation of the model, including a successful concept → pilot → fully scaled integration of a core business innovation with partner Lyft. The plan going forward is to fully scale and increase the size/quality of the pipeline of growth initiatives, partnerships, and investments.

3. **Specialized governance and shared incentives—Growth Board**

   CSAA IG has established an explicitly different approval and funding mechanism (separate from core business) for innovation and growth initiatives called the Growth Board. This addresses the common problem where innovation must compete with the core for funding and resources.

In addition, senior executives across the entire company share a common innovation goal (along with traditional business targets) as part of a three-year long-term incentive program. This reflects the core value of "acting as an enterprise owner" and mutually reinforces the importance of all executives to deliver across both core and innovation growth targets.

Perspective: Top Three Things Essential to CSAA S&I Development and Scale

1. **Vision and culture**

   With a mission to be there when members need them, and a vision to be members' first choice to life's uncertainties, CSAA is building an innovative company, not just an innovation department. CSAA IG is committed to being even more customer centric in how they design products and more agile in product development and speed to market. This is aligned with CSAA IG's mission and vision and builds on its already strong values-based, diverse, and inclusive culture.

2. **Balanced approach**

   Balance is crucial to CSAA IG's dual strategic imperatives to optimize and grow the core, and to place strategic bets for future growth and diversification. Permission to explore noncore insurance adjacencies, and to innovate outside of insurance all together, is counterbalanced by the commitment to partner with the core business to optimize and grow there as well.

3. **"Horizontal" perspective and emerging ecosystem access**

   The S&I team's wide lens and quality access into rapidly evolving marketplaces and intersecting tech/market ecosystems (sharing economy, data analysis/AI/machine learning, autonomous cars, blockchain) will impact current and future insurance businesses.

   With the launch of its new Silicon Valley office in early 2019, the S&I team plans to expand its engagement with the broader start-up and investor ecosystem and deepen its reputation as a corporate partner who delivers value to all stakeholders through commercial execution and value realization.

Best Example of How Business Model Works: Lyft

CSAA Insurance Group partnered with Lyft in 2017 to offer a simple but innovative offer to policyholders with an auto claim.

CSAA Insurance Group services more than half a million auto claims each year, most of which include rental vehicles. The process of securing a rental car can be time consuming and inconvenient for policyholders. To improve this experience for customers, CSAA Insurance Group piloted a program with Lyft—a first-of-its kind for both the insurance and ride-share industries. Eligible customers could choose to receive up to $200 in Lyft credits, in lieu of a rental car, while their personal car is being repaired. The pilot ran for approximately six months in Northern California. Goals of the pilot included:

- Improve customer experience by offering an alternative to the traditional rental car option
- Be a first mover and early adopter of a new option in auto claims
- Build a relationship with a leading global transportation network company

The pilot was a solid success, with high customer satisfaction and positive NPS scores. The company further partnered with Lyft on APIs to enable integration with our claims backend and have now scaled this offer across the entire CSAA IG footprint. The partnership with Lyft has expanded to new opportunities within CSAA IG and across AAA nationally.

How Is CSAA SI's Success Measured?

CSAA IG measures success in the following categories:

1. Building a customer-centric, innovative, and agile culture—key measures here include the innovation scores from our employee

engagement survey, total number of employee ideas generated/implemented and associated value created, number of employees participating in hackathons, etc.

2. Optimizing and growing our core—the key measures here are customer satisfaction/retention (NPS, market share), organic revenue growth, operational efficiency and savings from automation, AI, and machine learning.

3. Innovating our future—the key measures here are diversification (number of new businesses outside core) and "net new" revenue from those ventures. Includes new value propositions targeted at demographics we want to acquire at an accelerated rate (millennials, Gen-Z).

Across categories 2 and 3, the company tracks overall growth portfolio health as measured by number of opportunity areas and number of concepts in each, and by phase of development, throughput speed, and kill rates. In CVC, CSAA IG measures commercialization activity with portfolio companies, in addition to financial performance of the portfolio over time. Across all its efforts, CSAA IG assesses the quality of our partnerships and innovation leadership/positioning as measured by external press, impressions, and industry recognition/awards.

PROGRAM PROFILE: JETBLUE TECHNOLOGY VENTURES

Program Name	JetBlue Technology Ventures (JTV)
Date Established	January 2016
Parent HQ & CV Locations	JetBlue Airways–New York, NY JetBlue Technology Ventures–San Carlos, CA
Charter	JTV invests in, incubates, and partners with early-stage start-ups at the intersection of technology and travel to improve the end-to-end experience for travelers everywhere. We also address fundamental parent business priorities and provide curated learning opportunities to increase innovation for JetBlue. • 40% of focus is on technologies that can enhance JetBlue near term–within two years. • 60% of focus is longer-term impact on our parent company and industry–from 2 to 10 years in the future.
Legal Structure	• Independent subsidiary of JetBlue Airways, the parent company • Reports to JetBlue EVP and Chief Information Officer Eash Sundaram
CV Program Elements	• CVC–minority venture investing • Operations (CVBD/PMO)–facilitate and manage engagement with parent to drive strategic value capture from portfolio and CV team insights/perspectives • Discretionary pilot development
Team Size (12)	• JTV president Bonny Simi • CVC/Investment team (six people led by managing director, CA based) • Operations team (three people led by managing director; two embedded in parent NY HQ) • Communications Manager and Office Manager

Focus Areas	Five investment themes: 1. Seamless customer journey 2. Technology-powered magnificent service 3. Future of maintenance and operations 4. Innovation in distribution, revenue, and loyalty 5. Evolving regional travel
Program Scale	• Total # portfolio companies: 21 • Average # annual investments: 6–10 • Fund size: Typically seed/Series A/Series B investments funded from parent company balance sheet; total fund amount not disclosed
Recent Sample Investments	• ClimaCell (weather predicting/sensing) • Gladly (call center customer service platform) • SkyHour (digital gifting of travel) • Joby (electric vertical takeoff and landing aircraft for urban transit)
Select Syndicate Partners	• CVC: Intel Capital, Amadeus, Boeing Horizon X, Toyota AI, Verizon, AXA • VC: Canaan Partners, Crosslink, Greylock, NEA • Other: Plug & Play, TechStars

Description of Program Development Journey and Key Learnings

In early 2016, JetBlue Technology Ventures (JTV) launched in Silicon Valley with a mandate to improve the end-to-end experience for travelers everywhere and to help JetBlue stay ahead of industry developments. JTV was set up to identify and support innovation opportunities in the travel, transportation, and hospitality industries that look two, five, and ten years down the road. JTV prioritizes investments that align with five original investment themes (see above) and has its eye on emerging technologies such as AI, machine learning, electric propulsion, and blockchain.

With an eye to accelerating development, JTV president and JetBlue veteran Bonny Simi launched the CVC unit by tapping into a network of top venture capital and investment firm leaders to learn firsthand about best practice program elements and ecosystem-driven implementation models that could be adapted for JTV and JetBlue. JTV's program execution strategy was to "think big, start small, build fast," with continuous testing, refinement, and incremental expansion through experience going forward.

Key JTV Program Design Elements

- **End-to-end investing model**

  The JTV team is a group of investors who understand Silicon Valley and venture capital combined with operators who are embedded at JetBlue to remain closely connected with the mother ship company and industry. This mix of investing specialists and operations professionals allows for streamlined engagement between JTV and JetBlue. The blended team has built a track record as an impact delivery engine, optimizing deal flow and facilitating introductions based on JetBlue business priorities.

- **Creative parent engagement**

  In addition to bringing JetBlue start-up opportunities aligned to the five investment themes, JTV also designed and runs a signature collaborative innovation program with different JetBlue business units to help them maintain a fresh outlook on the future. These programs are twelve-week JTV-driven engagements where JTV helps the business unit understand what the future of their sector looks like. JTV casts a wide net to find a large group of start-ups that fit within the engagement's theme and then thoughtfully reviews and whittles down the list to a handful of start-ups that pitch to JetBlue leaders for potential partnerships or proof-of-concept tests.

- **Ecosystem partnerships**

    There's a natural ceiling on JetBlue's ability to operationally absorb proof of concepts and partner with emerging technologies each year. To address this challenge, JTV is building a global network of like-minded travel industry providers (e.g., airlines, hotels) who value JTV's emerging market insights and are prepared to operationally engage with quality portfolio companies. The first partner is Air New Zealand, which has seconded a person to JTV's offices to immerse in the local deal flow and portfolio.

Other JTV Success Factors and Uniqueness

- **Structure as separate legal entity**—JTV operates independently from parent company.
    o Benefit to parent company JetBlue: JTV's budget is disclosed, but not part of JetBlue's operating cost. This also offers some legal protection.
    o Benefit to JTV: JetBlue has twenty-two thousand people and traditional, mature processes. Without operating in this type of bureaucracy, JTV is able to have an agile and adaptable business environment that makes it quicker and nimbler.
- **Commitment to continuous program improvement**—Build, test, and actively refine elements.
    o In certain cases, JTV expanded activities by up-leveling and building out the JetBlue-embedded operations team. The growth has been very successful to drive proof of concepts and integrations.
    o At the same time, JTV has stepped away from pre-seed-stage and accelerator investing when it determined its value was uncertain.
    o JTV also revisits its investment themes every year in February, to ensure focus remains on the areas that matter most to JetBlue.

- **External reputation**—Industry leadership positioning and program expansion.
  - o The JTV team spends a considerable amount of time speaking at events to share its travel vision and insights, contributing to the broader innovation ecosystem and furthering the innovative external brand of JetBlue.
  - o JTV has quickly built a reputation for its ability to attract and leverage like-minded and complementary companies interested in innovation partnering and co-investment opportunities in high-quality start-ups (e.g., Intel Capital, Toyota AI Ventures, Qantas Ventures, Boeing HorizonX, Verizon Ventures).

Best Example of How Business Model Works: ClimaCell

ClimaCell is a weather technology company that provides high-definition weather forecasting tools to businesses and governments worldwide and offers instant access to actionable, street-level weather data in real time. The solution helps companies make better business decisions by more accurately predicting the weather.

JetBlue Technology Ventures built a business relationship with ClimaCell when it was still in its seed stage of development. JTV envisioned the application of ClimaCell's service in the aviation sector, and JetBlue trialed the solution for six months at Boston's Logan Airport to assist with lightning, fog, and snow predictions. The trial improved ground operations and safety and reduced costs associated with unnecessary cancellations and delays. Shortly afterward, when ClimaCell was raising its next round of financing, JTV invested along with other partners. JTV built broad awareness of JetBlue's pilot and made introductions throughout the aviation industry, leading to accelerated interest from other aviation stakeholders. JetBlue itself expanded ClimaCell's technology to airports in New York, Fort Lauderdale, Orlando, Newark, and Washington, DC. Presently, JTV is helping ClimaCell expand its proof of concepts to international markets.

ClimaCell's relationship with JTV has been critical to additional funding. ClimaCell's success story with JetBlue serves as an impactful reference, and JTV is an ongoing proponent of the ClimaCell platform, business model, and growth projections for other present and prospective investors.

Perspective: Top Three Things Essential to JTV's Development and Scale

1. **Vision**
   - From its inception, JTV has had a vision-driven charter, structure, program plan, and an eighteen-month implementation roadmap.
   - The JTV team has deep expertise in aviation and also specializes in hospitality, regional transportation, operations, and more. This leads to an insight- and ecosystem-informed strategic plan.
2. **Team structure**
   - JTV's mix of independence coupled with high-level oversight allows for a nimble operating unit that can move quickly at the pace of Silicon Valley, while also ensuring alignment with the current and future needs of JetBlue.
   - The team's blend of investors in Silicon Valley that sources start-ups with operators at JetBlue headquarters drives customer adaptation and stays in tune to the parent company's business strategy and culture.
3. **Expanding ecosystem**
   - The June 2018 launch of an international partnership program allows JTV to connect start-ups with partner airlines and hospitality groups as potential customers and investors—providing further value to start-up and industry stakeholders.

How Is JTV Measured?

JTV's success is measured in three ways:

1. **Near term:** Successful proof of concepts and implementation of new technologies that enhance JetBlue's innovative culture, bottom line, operations and safety, or customer experience.
2. **Midterm:** Market intelligence and knowledge gained from having a seat at the table in emerging technologies.
3. **Long term:** Financial returns from successful investments.

JTV seeks to demonstrate significant strategic impact within two years and modest financial returns within seven. With respect to the strategic impact, several proof of concepts and portfolio company integrations have already demonstrated results for JetBlue and were featured during JetBlue's 2018 Investor Day presentation.

CHAPTER 4

Expansion Phase (Years 4–6)

The Goal: Obtain parent commitment for program step-up/continuation—funding, people, operating reach. ("The Ask")

What's Happening:

- **Focus**: Refinement of portfolio strategy and approach for program expansion
- **Operating style**: Dedicated professional team, institutionalized end-to-end investing platform
- **Performance**: Demonstration of program momentum and internal/external credibility

The Challenge: *How to demonstrate CV program strategic relevance and make case for program expansion/continuation, while retaining and growing unique high-performance specialist CV team.*

Executive Summary

Years four to six are often a pivot point for the future of a CV program, which typically has been able to fly under the radar in its early days and now must compete internally and often externally for significant resources. Does it:

- Survive corporate strategy and management shifts?
- Continue to expand within the parent?
- Spin out as path to stepped-up funding and greater freedom to operate, plus diversification of risk, reduction of internal operating friction and other CV program growth inhibitors?
- Wind down, cut back, or focus on management of an existing portfolio?

It is a critical period for testing both the operational readiness of the CV program to scale predictably, as well as its ability to meet portfolio performance expectations that justify corporate parent appetite for higher levels of dedicated funding, more autonomy, and a more visible CV role in corporate innovation strategy direction setting. At the same time, it is a review of the parent's status, and strength of commitment to the CV program.

It's all about growth options—for the CV program and for the parent. There is no foregone conclusion about what these options should be and how they should be shaped (back to the program design principle that one size never fits all). The framing of viable expansion funding options—internal, external, hybrid—is informed by a combination of factors including team skill set, program track record/momentum and parent perception of strategic relevance in conjunction with current parent company circumstances.

High Performer Hallmarks

1. **Agility in refining strategic investment theses/portfolio focus** with demonstrated path to impact and value delivery
2. **Custom recruitment/retention plan for high performance CV team** that includes both senior investment (CVC) and portfolio/business development (CVBD) professionals

3. **Institutionalization of the CV operating platform**: End-to-end investing processes, streamlined governance, performance reporting, and automation.

Seasoned CV teams continually test their vision and charter through market experience and through engagement with internal business and functional partners, using impactful wins to refine their portfolio focus.

Programs with established portfolios (e.g., ten to fifteen companies) and early wins build on momentum and extend core CV program with a formalized CVBD function designed to enable scaling, maximize portfolio performance, and drive impact.

In addition, design for CV program scale and sustainability drives need to streamline, map, document, automate, and measure key processes and activities.

Threats and Antibodies

Amplifying the CV program and portfolio development brings more internal/external exposure just as the complexity of program elements and operating pressures that must be managed is increasing. And with accelerated programs, the amount of time for operating under the radar is reduced, forcing CV teams to compete earlier for internal mindshare, funding, and resources. Key challenges include:

- **The shifting sands of the corporate parent**

    Typical parent company executive rotations, corporate strategy shifts, and reorganizations compound the risk for CV program development at this point of expansion (changing goals/governance/lack of alignment in what defines adequately "impactful" program performance)

    o   Internal: When CVC leader/team must "start over" to (re)build internal credibility, reporting and other key relationships, in order to reestablish effective governance and regain freedom to operate at the previous pace, with fully functioning CV program charter, team, tool sets, and committed lineup of essential internal resources so essential for enabling portfolio company—parent corporation connections, strategic leverage, and accelerated commercial value.

o External: Internal changes/delays can quickly undermine CV program/team external credibility, the ability of the CV team to deliver on early performance goals and compete at pace on the outside for deal flow, for "anchor" portfolio investments, for best syndicate/portfolio and innovation partners, and for critical ecosystem positioning in quickly evolving new markets. (Note: Given the current acceleration rate of CV program/portfolio development and ecosystem partnering imperatives/partner agreements, the potential for CV program losses are much broader, more dramatic and very public.)

- **The compensation conundrum**

  For most CV programs, investment goals are a combination of strategic impact and financial return. This has historically created a compensation conundrum for recruiting, rewarding, and retaining CV professional talent—how to frame CV compensation relative to both traditional venture capital risk-reward models and established corporate salary structures. In years four to six in the development of a CV program, retention of high-performance senior individuals and expansion of the team can become a challenge, particularly when the team as a unit meets early program performance goals, putting real pressure on compensation package value and career path definition.

- **The "Fund"**

  Accelerated program expansion often requires more corporate funding earlier, if portfolio momentum is to be maintained. This increases the risk for young programs that don't yet have a fully realized track record to persuade parents to increase investment dollars (at the expense of other corporate priorities) and provide the multiyear commitments (a.k.a. the "Fund") that partners and portfolio companies expect to see.

Expansion Phase Design Rules
Charter

1. **Reassess and refine CV program charter and portfolio strategy**

   Seasoned teams continually test their charters and investment theses both through market experience and through engagement with internal business and functional partners, using impactful "wins" to refine investment priorities.

   With established portfolios of at least ten to fifteen companies, CV teams in this phase often have demonstrated the ability to deploy variable-size investments (small to large) with various program tools (investment, portfolio development, etc.), and can refine/rebalance portfolio strategies to reflect impact goals.

   Forward-looking programs, such as Merck Global Health Innovation (GHI) at this point in its development, may employ "market maker" strategies and tools to execute on a portfolio vision and accelerate impact with investment/ecosystem partnering targets, a broader investment toolkit (PE, M&A), and the ability to make bigger bets.

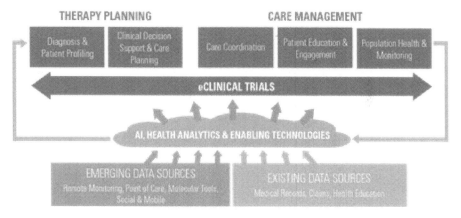

Figure 1: Merck GHI—Ecosystem Vision for Portfolio and Partnering Strategy (source: GHI Website)

2. **Define options and roadmap for CV program expansion**

Emerging market insights and fast wins with clear impact for all stakeholders serve as early proof points for key program execution capabilities (e.g., strategic landscaping/ecosystem modeling; end-to-end investing approach) and lay a foundation for consideration of expansion options, including:

- More BU/functional partnerships targeting the same focus areas
- New BU/functional partnerships targeting new focus areas
- New focus areas
- New geographies
- Specialized fund participation/partnerships and a managed program for expansion (e.g. to geos, specialized domains, seed stage investments)

Insurance giant Munich Re has expanded its CV program across multiple vectors by establishing a "CV platform" that allows the team to efficiently spin up new investment focus themes/areas and dedicated "funds" for new BU partners. (See Munich Re Ventures' profile at the end of chapter 4.)

3. **Evaluate funding options for CV program continuity/scale**

By the end of year four, initial CVC allocations ("Fund 1") are often largely invested so a program faces a critical pivot point, during which a step-up in exposure and funding is required if the program is to deliver on its vision for strategic impact.

The CV program must drive development of strategy, negotiation, and resolution with parent regarding program trajectory, funding, and next steps. Options typically include the following:

- Continue to expand program within the parent (annual or multiyear formal allocation)
- Spin out as a means to diversify risk, improve freedom to operate, reduce corporate friction and CV program growth inhibitors (sole LP or multi-LP)
- Wind down, cut back, or focus solely on management of the existing portfolio (no growth funding)

Evaluation of "spin" options may surface as a critical decision matrix at this phase with teams facing CVC "battle fatigue."

Many have considered, but most haven't spun out after analyzing all options rank-ordered by strength of rationale/trade-offs for all stakeholders, relative lead times to development, and management complexity.

Often, the most realistic option is a "hybrid" (remain internal/ corporate owned and have a position in an external fund; or create collaboration as LP with multiple BU partners and/or other complementary corporates/ecosystem partners). (See Factors Determining CV Program Spin-Readiness at the back of chapter 4 Design Rules.)

Echo Health Ventures, a multi-LP spin-out funded by Cambia Health Solutions and Mosaic Health Solutions (Blue Cross Blue Shield providers based in the Pacific Northwest and North Carolina), represents a unique risk-reduced approach to CV program expansion—spinning out investing activity while maintaining embedded linkages to parent. (See Echo Profile at the end of chapter 4.)

Process

4. **Review and streamline CV program governance**

    By the end of year three, a CV team has likely faced at least one change in reporting, a corporate strategy shift and/or a reorganization, and has identified investment decision-making barriers—all tests of program adaptability and agility.

    Recent trends show that trusted, experienced teams that can demonstrate early CV successes are buffering their programs with increased CVC leader/team signatory authority and operational autonomy, and by streamlining deal management processes and investment committee (IC) decision-making.

    In some cases, seasoned CV teams are acting more like VC partnerships in reviewing potential investments with a final signature required only for larger deals. For example, Microsoft's M12 ventures requires a single signature from the EVP Business Development for final deal approval.

5. **Define CVBD ("landing") process and align/integrate with CVC ("investment") process**

    Leading programs with established portfolios and early strategic wins are building on momentum and extending the CVC function with a formalized CVBD function designed to enable scaling, maximize portfolio performance, and drive impact.

    This means mapping, documenting, and measuring end-to-end investing processes with clarified ownership, roles, and resourcing among the CV team (CVC + CVBD) and the corporate parent (BUs, functions). This also requires that the CVBD process is architected, tested, and supported with venture-appropriate engagement tools and resources (PMO, MoU, PoC/Pilot, JDA, license, etc.)

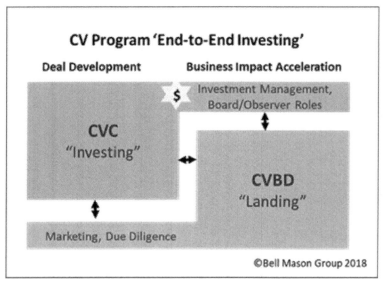

Figure 2: End-to-end investing (sourcing to landing spot)

6. **Identify key success factors and solve for barriers to portfolio company landing spots**

    Start-ups in complex, regulated industries like health care, financial services, and insurance increasingly believe the ability to deliver the power of the corporate parent's ecosystem position, customer base, and operational knowledge/expertise can make capable strategic corporate investors more attractive than many of their institutional investor (VC/PE) peers.

Health Evolution Corporate Venture Group (HE-CVG)–Key success factors for impactful corporate parent/portfolio company engagement

- **Strategic alignment:** Parent priorities and CVC investment portfolio
- **Parent executive sponsorship:** C-Suite/BU support and involvement
- **CVC portfolio/market development function** to drive:
  - Portfolio evangelism
  - Parent critical need/portfolio company offer matching (deep knowledge of both)
  - Facilitation of big company/small company expectation setting
- **BU/functional prerequisites:**
  - Portfolio company tie-in to strategic initiative
  - Partnership mindset
  - Value-focused point of contact/owner
  - Venture PMO/execution expertise to drive adoption plan
- **Portfolio company prerequisites:**
  - Focus on priority sector for CVC parent
  - Dedicated PMO, (key) account management

Source: 2018 Survey (HE-CVG/Liz Arrington–BMG)

However, barriers to parent/portfolio company engagement can be significant: for example, parent-portfolio solution and operational impedance mismatches, lack of committed resources (staff, money, expertise, PMO), and parent conflicts of interest (e.g., investor vs. commercializer, competitive investments).

Furthermore, programs like Munich Re Ventures and Capital One Growth Ventures (following the In-Q-Tel "gold standard" example) have proactively addressed potential barriers with structured

BU and portfolio company "onboarding" processes and formalized parent linkages (e.g., strategy development collaboration, integrated investment/venture development processes and metrics, money, and specialized staffing/resource commitments to support investments).

Team

7. **Develop and integrate CV business development (CVBD) function/ team**

   As CV portfolios reach critical mass, CVBD frequently moves from an investment professional responsibility or a BU-seconded high performer role to a formalized parallel function and dedicated team led by a senior professional "peer" to the CVC leader. (See Sample CVBD Leader job description box.)

CVBD Leader—VP and/or Managing Director

Senior leader responsible for CVBD function/program design and portfolio development and management, including overall management of dedicated CVBD team, creation/maintenance of internal corporate and external ecosystem networks and relationships, and facilitation of business partnering arrangements for portfolio companies. Also includes responsibility for creation and management of CV Unit strategic marketing plan and programs, strategic communications (internal and external facing), and ongoing operational support for CV Unit /portfolio companies. Works with CVC investment team to deliver on "end-to-end investing" model, with goal of accelerating portfolio/portfolio co. value and making parent co. strategic leverage and "impact performance" more concrete and measurable.

Key responsibilities include:

- Work with CVC unit leader and team's investment professionals to integrate strategic innovation/CV business development activities and processes into the unit's end-to-end investing charter and operations

---

- Guide and help actively develop portfolio co./parent business engagement
  - Work with portfolio companies to help identify and map potential high-value points of business synergy with the parent corp. (e.g., targeted points in business units, functions, customers, external ecosystem partners)
  - Drive portfolio co introductions/business pitches/relationship management, aligning portfolio co. needs and parent business goals and motivations via participating internal corporate decision makers and corporate implementation teams (up to and including incentive structures)
- Work with portfolio companies to identify and develop pitches for external points of potential business leverage and ecosystem partnering/business collaboration opportunities
- Drive definition and refinement of unit's strategic performance metrics and milestones; develop systems to "fast-track" strategic progress against goals (with data collection and reporting to be designed for automation)
- Oversee marketing team that manages networking events, press coverage, and (internal/external) marketing activities designed to generate awareness and increase quality deal flow and value of internal/external CVBD professionals' networks

Experience: 15+ years of experience and track record in corporate venturing, deal making, partnering, corporate development, and/or business development roles. Advanced business degree and may have relevant technology education and previous roles in emerging business operations.

Although the levels and construct of specialist CVBD/portfolio development teams vary widely by CV program charter and objectives, as well as by the degree of support from the parent BUs/functions, key portfolio development team capabilities often include the following:

- Business/portfolio development (CVBD)
- Market domain/technical/scientific SMEs

- Marketing and communications
- Project management (PMO)

These capabilities are defined and resourced within the CV team, through parent BU and functional partnerships, and in some cases are outsourced to specialists.

As a reference point, Microsoft's M12 Ventures reports to Peggy Johnson, EVP for business development, with nearly half of the team in portfolio support roles. Every portfolio company is assigned a portfolio development professional to find engagement opportunities, navigate Microsoft, and support venture scaling.

8. **Develop CV team recruitment and retention program (compensation and career paths)**

Corporate venturing is a network-driven business: getting into high-quality deals and landing them impactfully within the parent depends on CV professionals' relationships. Top CV programs strive to hold senior team members for at least three to five years to ensure uninterrupted portfolio momentum, expansion, and delivery of strategic/financial impact.

> Note: Thelander Investment Firm Compensation research provides compensation benchmarks for investment talent across CVC peers, institutional investment firms (VC, PE), and private companies.
>
> Titles and compensation benchmarks for portfolio development professionals are beginning to emerge, with Thelander CV compensation research probing these roles for the first time in 2018.

Corporate willingness to evolve HR structures to institutionalize CV-specific roles with competitive compensation packages, titling, career paths, and succession planning is a test of ongoing commitment to the program. Strong CVC financial performance (exits) combined with key team member recruitment and retention challenges may open the door for discussion of competitive (upside) compensation approaches in addition to strategic performance-linked bonus schemes. And with team expansion may come the need for CV-specific career tracks outside the existing corporate HR/business banding.

Innovation Partnering

9. **Develop high-performance portfolio and innovation partnering program**

   A key element of an impactful CV initiative is a high-performance innovation partnering program built on a compelling ecosystem vision and a CV program reputation for quality, investment professionalism, and the proven ability to deliver parent resources and facilitate commercial relationships.

   These programs, typically managed by the Portfolio Development/CVBD function, are the foundation for building

   • Internal networks: Broadening reach and engagement

     Leverage early wins to expand internal partnership programs targeting both senior executive/sponsor champions and the middle management owners needed to drive commercial/operational relationships with portfolio companies. Note: A 2018 survey of Health Evolution CVG members showed that when evaluating potential CVC co-investors, a program's track record in facilitating portfolio company/parent engagement was seen to be nearly as important as direct investing track record and even more important than market/tech domain expertise.

   • External networks: Expanding access to and facilitating engagement with quality portfolio companies, co-investors and business partners

     Execute on shift from ad hoc investments to synergistic focus area/ecosystem portfolios and explore partnerships/co-investment "clubs" with complementary CVCs, institutional investors, and business ecosystem members. Note: CVCs are increasingly co-investing with other corporates for horizontal technology, applications, or platform development, even though their parent companies may view each other as competitors.

Performance

10. **Up-level CV portfolio management function and refine CV program performance framework**

    Years four to six are the test period for a CV program: Can it meet portfolio strategy and execution goals, achieve credible financial returns, demonstrate measurable strategic impact, recruit/retain a high-performance team, and establish a predictable, streamlined operating platform?

    As CV portfolios grow to ten to fifteen companies and feel pressure to demonstrate measurable business/strategic impact, CV programs often up-level the portfolio management function/leadership to play a strategic role beyond basic finance and administration.

A key focus of the **Portfolio Management** function is to develop a CV program performance management framework that both resonates with the parent and integrates the following:

- Financial metrics–demonstration of investor quality
  - Portfolio IRR, cash-on-cash returns, exits
  - Other people's money (OPM) as an indicator of deal syndicate partner quality and power
- Strategic metrics–delivery on charter objectives, measurable business impact
  - End-to-end investing waterfall percentages to track parent engagement and assess strategic relevance and potential impact of portfolio
  - Commercial impact: revenues, operating efficiencies/cost savings, risk reduction, new markets/customers
  - Market/technology ecosystem insights
  - Parent innovation brand, culture change
- Operational metrics–CV platform development milestones and quality indicators (institutionalize/automate–measure key processes and activities)

While the charters for most CV programs are strategic, the performance lingua franca of their parent corporations is financial (quarter-to-quarter versus longer venture capital time frames). CV financial performance is the easiest thing to measure, and important for external investor credibility, but in most cases, even very good financial returns won't move the needle for the parent corporation, and they fail to reflect the strategic value delivered.

The Portfolio Management function drives the tracking/dashboarding process and reporting calendar (weekly, monthly, quarterly, annual), balancing data needed by the CV team with parent-appropriate executive communications and program performance indicators.

Early on, the Capital One Growth Ventures team took the cultural pulse of the parent and concluded that they needed to be quantitative in decision-making and reporting. They designed and formalized an evaluation and portfolio performance tracking system that measures both financial, strategic, and cultural impact scores at both portfolio and CV partner levels.

11. **Use strategic stakeholder communications program to drive CV value perception and leadership positioning**

With increasing program visibility, strategic communications become a critical business tool for educating, demonstrating CV performance/value, and maintaining "touch" and productive connections with corporate parent and other stakeholders. (See Sample CV Program Marketing Plan.)

A primary goal is to demonstrate CV program quality with validated investment ecosystem positioning that highlights program potential for strategic leverage and impact in addition to early financial performance (exits).

Figure 3: Capital One Growth Ventures' strategic value scoring

Case studies go a long way to validate/communicate CV program "more than money" positioning/value to parent, portfolio companies, and syndicate partners.

Sample CV Program Marketing Plan

Plan Element	Description/Examples
Positioning/Charter	• Program charter • Elevator pitch and message model for consistent content and communications
External Audiences, Ecosystem Model	Layered model of categories (potential partners, investment focus areas) of opinion leaders, influencers, partners, and key participants (potential advisors)
Internal Audiences	Specific group and individual communication targets
Modular Presentation, Tools	Ten- to fifteen-slide core presentation can be tailored for internal and external audiences, partners, ecosystem targets; strategy video, white paper(s); end-to-end case studies
Internal Programs	Internal presentations and white papers; sector "demo" days; innovation network; leverage of corporate vehicles/events, newsletters, intranets, regular email "pulses," feedback with champions/stakeholders
External Programs	Website (with submission form), CEO summit, conferences, speaking, blogs, sponsorships, press releases (charter/launch, personnel, funding, exits), ecosystem road show
Calendar, Key Events, Milestones	Consolidated view of unit initiatives, industry and relevant corporate events, and milestone commitments
Measurement/ Tuning	Annual survey of internal and external audiences to asses impact and gather input and ideas for next phase plan
Resources, Budget	Program owners, internal resources needed, budget for programs, external events, services

Factors Determining CV Program Spin-Readiness

Factor	Rating (H-M-L)	Comments
Strategic relevance of CVC program to parent		• Drives degree of executive commitment to CVC • Informs desire to keep inside vs. spin (low = spin)
Parent's corporate performance		• Up cycles benefit CVC: brand value (recruiting, partnering), cash, RSU value for comp • Down cycles negatively impact investment, brand
CVC program performance		• Success increases likelihood of CVC access to additional capital (outside and in) • Performance drives attractiveness of team for external poaching (by other CVCs, VCs/PE) • Market perspective on CVC unit quality informs parent desire to keep inside vs. spin
Parent ability/ willingness to fund significant strategic investment in noncore areas (adjacent, emerging, horizontal, market platform, competitive, etc.)		• Informs ability of team to continue to execute on proven investment business model • May open door for fund collaborations with partners (inside or outside parent)
Parent HR flexibility		• Unique CVC professional track (titles, bands, comp) • Competitiveness with investment ecosystem peer benchmarks (CVC, VC, Private Co): base, bonus, upside ("pay for performance") levers • Standing headcount allocations per strategic plan

Expansion Phase Design Rules

Charter	1. Re-assess and refine CV program charter and portfolio strategy 2. Define options and roadmap for CV program expansion 3. Evaluate funding options for CV program continuity/scale
Process	4. Review, streamline CV program governance 5. Define CVBD ("landing") process and align/integrate with CVC ("investment") process 6. Identify key success factors, solve for barriers to portfolio company 'landing'
Team	7. Develop and integrate CV business development (CVBD) function/team 8. Develop CV team recruitment and retention program (compensation and career paths)
Innovation Partnering	9. Develop high performance portfolio and innovation partnering program
Performance	10. Up-level CV portfolio management function and refine CV program performance framework 11. Use strategic stakeholder communications program to drive CV value perception and leadership positioning

HIGH PERFORMER PROFILES
Expansion Phase (Years 4–6)
PROGRAM PROFILE: ECHO HEALTH VENTURES

Program Name	Echo Health Ventures
Date Established	2016 spinout combining existing CVC programs of Cambia Health Solutions (Direct Health Solutions) and Blue Cross North Carolina's subsidiary, Mosaic Health Solutions, into new Joint Venture focused on strategic investment
Parent HQ & CV Locations	Parents: Cambia Health Solutions, also parent to parent to Regence BCBS Plans in WA, OR, ID, and UT (Portland, OR), Blue Cross NC's subsidiary, Mosaic Health Solutions (Durham, NC) CV Program Locations: Portland, OR; Durham, NC; Seattle, WA
Charter	Create an industry-leading corporate investment platform by building a diverse portfolio of health care-technology and services companies that support Cambia's and BCNC's commitments to transformative, consumer-centric health care and to drive financial value.
Legal, Reporting Structure	• Joint Venture reporting to board made up of members of Cambia and Blue Cross NC boards of directors • LLC (but balance sheet allocation vs. "Fund") • Reports to the boards of Cambia and Mosaic
CV Program Elements	• Strategic minority equity investing (CVC) • Market development (CVBD) • Ability to make control investments • Support parent companies with corporate development and business development services
Team Size	• Leadership (2)– CEO (Rob Coppedge) and COO (Michael Mankowski) • CVC (9, headed by COO reporting to CEO) • Market development (6, headed by MD reporting to CEO) • Admin and operations (4) • External advisors and advisory board

Focus Areas	• Health-care information technology • Health-care services • Digital health
Program Scale	• Total # portfolio companies: 26 • Average # annual investments: 3–6 • Stage agnostic–focus on venture and growth equity with ability to participate in larger private equity if highly strategic • Evergreen structure; total capital access not disclosed
Recent Sample Investments	• Avalon: Redefines the way health plans, physicians, and laboratories coordinate laboratory care. The company provides a comprehensive program that manages outpatient laboratory services across all providers, including independent, physician office, and hospital-based labs. Using an independent Clinical Advisory Board (CAB), Avalon has developed a suite of science-based lab policies addressing all lab testing categories. These policies are administered through proprietary, automated technology to remove inappropriate utilization and typically save health plans and TPAs 7 to 12% on outpatient lab spend. • Livongo: Empowers people with chronic conditions to live better and healthier lives by addressing various chronic conditions. The company's team of data scientists aggregate and interpret substantial amounts of health data and information to create actionable, personalized, and timely health signals. • Phreesia: Engages patients in their care and provides a modern, consistent intake experience, while enabling healthcare organizations to optimize their staffing and enhance clinical care. Phreesia manages intake for over 70 million patients annually across its rapidly expanding network, and the company has checked in more than 15 percent of the US population since its inception.

	• AccessOne: Provides consumer-friendly patient financing programs in partnership with hospital systems by offering patients low- and zero-interest loans for the "self-pay" portion of medical expenses. The company provides an easy-to-use patient portal, enabling patients to pay their medical bills online, and grants equal access to everyone interested, regardless of a patient's credit history.
Select Syndicate Partners	• CVC: Blue Venture Fund, Celgene, Amgen, Providence Ventures • VC: HLM, Health Enterprise Partners, Cardinal Partners, Noro Moseley, LRV Health, Hatteras Venture Partners, Town Hall Ventures, Healthquest • PE: Abry Partners, LLR Partners, Nautic Partners

Description of Program Development Journey and Key Learnings

The 2016 launch of Echo Health Ventures was the result of growth and synergies between two established and like-minded corporate venture units: Cambia Health Solutions, a not-for-profit total health solutions company whose Regence regional health plans are a member of the BlueCross BlueShield Association; and Mosaic Health Solutions, the investment arm of BlueCross North Carolina (also a not-for profit member of BlueCross BlueShield Association).

Cambia and BCNC had separately formed corporate venture units, in 2010 and 2014, respectively, to accelerate transformation across the healthcare ecosystem. Over time, each program had begun transitioning from their foundational start-up phases (years zero to three), to sustainable programs that were beginning to deliver meaningful impact for both their corporate parents and portfolio companies (years four to six). Early experience across both firms pointed to the value of corporate venturing and demonstrated early success through partnerships between their portfolio companies and parent organizations.

Simultaneously, each unit had also experienced several barriers in the formative years, driving the need for more formalized structures across the investment and market development functions. Given that both teams had similar investment processes and parent partnership dynamics, it was a logical next step to begin exploring how to scale efforts and work more closely together. As a result, Echo Health Ventures was founded by spinning out the two separate units and forming a new joint venture investment platform that is co-owned by both Cambia and BCNC. Established in late 2016, Echo is now focused on building a diverse portfolio of health-care technology and services companies that support both Cambia's and BCNC's commitments to transformative, consumer-centric health care, while also driving financial value across the combined portfolios.

Today, Echo comprises a team of approximately fifteen investment and market development professionals, with offices in Durham, Seattle, and Portland. Under the leadership of Rob Coppedge, CEO and twenty-plus-year veteran in health-care investing, the program has grown to incorporate twenty-five portfolio companies across the health-care IT and health-care services sectors. Echo is a stage-agnostic, strategic health-care investor, with preference for leading deals alongside experienced and like-minded syndicate partners. Echo has invested in companies ranging from seed through mature stages, with check sizes ranging from $750,000 to $20 million, respectively. While Echo's typical investment stage falls with the early to growth phase, the firm's top priority is to invest in strong companies and management teams that are demonstrably addressing critical issues within the broader healthcare landscape and for Echo's two parent organizations.

Key Echo Program Design Elements

- **Market development**

    One of Echo's core differentiators is its market development model, which has created an innovative workforce of individuals with expertise in both strategic investing and business development. Prior to launching Echo, business development functions at each parent generated both successful outcomes and lessons learned, all of which helped inform the market development model and strategy upon Echo's formation. Today the team maintains strategic relationships and processes across the entire organization of each parent, and each of Echo's portfolio companies. These capabilities have enabled Echo to better understand the detailed strategies and decision-making processes at each parent, ultimately driving stronger investment theses and portfolio management proficiencies.

- **Investment strategy**

    Echo's investment strategy comprises five key investment themes that are core to helping the healthcare industry transform to a quality-based, cost-effective system that is oriented around the consumer. These themes are at the forefront in the evaluation of each new potential investment. This focus has enabled the firm to develop scalable processes and expertise in critical subsectors of healthcare that will clearly accelerate the strategies of Echo's parent organizations.

- **Scalable investment platform**

  Echo has spent considerable time building professional investment and market development teams, developing standardized processes, and implementing appropriate tools that drive quick decision-making and workflows in all facets of the business. This has helped Echo form a scalable model that is able to move more quickly on investment and partnership decisions than is typical of many incumbent CVCs.

Other Success Factors and Uniqueness

- **Culture**

  Prior to its launch, Echo's leadership spent considerable time developing a robust strategy around its culture, how it would recruit and retain talent across the organization, and how each member of the team would support both Echo's portfolio companies and its two parent organizations. The firm is dedicated to a culture of transparency, accountability, and humility across all facets of the organization. Echo's early focus on these values have helped the firm strengthen its reputation in the market, through strong partnerships across management teams, syndicate investors, board governance, and all levels of the organization at both Cambia and BCNC.

Best Example of How Business Model Works: Livongo

Livongo empowers people with chronic conditions, such as diabetes, to treat their condition on a single tech-enabled platform. The company combines a digital device that monitors blood glucose, monitoring services, and access to a diabetes coach to determine and intervene when blood glucose levels become dangerously high or low for an individual.

In early 2018, Echo began sourcing chronic disease management investment opportunities in support of Cambia's strategy to reduce the high costs associated with chronic disease. Echo ultimately invested in Livongo, given the company's unique approach to diabetes prevention and treatment and its compelling market traction. Simultaneously, Echo began facilitating introductions and driving relationships between stakeholders at Livongo and Cambia.

Through this leadership, Cambia and Livongo began to scope a commercial contract, and form a strategy that would implement Livongo's capabilities across Cambia's regional health plans. Within a relatively short time frame, a contract was signed, securing Livongo as Cambia's partner of choice in addressing chronic conditions. While still early, Cambia is eager to work with Livongo on building out additional programs in the future. While many CVCs often make introductions between portfolio companies and parents, the real value of this relationship was with the ongoing support that Echo provided to each entity. Given Echo's familiarity with Cambia's vision and corporate structure, the market development team was able to ensure that the right conversations were happening across all levels of the organization at the right time. As an example, Michael Sturmer, Livongo's SVP of health services, said that the value of the relationship was Echo's depth in supporting the company navigate Cambia, stating, "All investors make introductions. But they don't all have the resources to curate relationships into something foundational. It is tremendously valuable for Echo's market development team to match us with the right people at Cambia. If we understand how our solution fits within their vision, we can think more strategically about how to help. Their business development approach is truly best practice among investors."

Perspective: Top Three Things Deemed Essential to Program's Development and Scale

1. Like any investment firm, Echo's ability to scale will depend largely on its ability to generate portfolio returns and deliver strategic value to its portfolio companies. Echo has implemented strong underwriting and portfolio governance practices that ensure the firm is making smart investment decisions and is supporting its existing portfolio appropriately. As Echo matures, it will need to ensure that its team and underwriting processes can scale with the business.

2. Echo's ultimate success will be driven by its ability to carry out its vision to build a portfolio that both drives financial value and

supports Cambia's and BCNC's commitments to transformative, consumer-centric health care. Echo must continue building and executing on strong relationships with its parent organizations, through the work of its market development team. As each parent organization adjusts to market fluctuations, adjustments in leadership, and shifts in strategies, it will be critical for Echo to maintain its operational integration and strong relationships across each entity.

3. One of Echo's key success factors has been strong executive leadership support from each of its parent entities. Echo's investment committee comprises both CEOs and CFOs from Cambia and BCNC. Additionally, its board is made up of board members from both Cambia's and BCNC's board of directors. Echo's success is largely dependent on having the buy-in and support from top-level leadership at each parent, which ultimately helps drive partnerships and successes across all levels of each entity. Echo must continue to be focused on maintaining these core relationships in order to build a portfolio of companies that are in line with parent strategies.

How Is Echo Health Ventures Measured?

Echo is measured on two key metrics: the IRR it generates through its portfolio and its ability to create meaningful partnerships between Echo's parent organizations and portfolio companies. The firm has created a proprietary ROI model that measures the associated value generated through each partnership, with incentives aligned accordingly. Additionally, Echo, Cambia, and BCNC have each built a strong infrastructure that encourages strong collaboration and accountability for tracking and meeting partnership expectations.

PROGRAM PROFILE: MUNICH RE VENTURES

Program Name	Munich Re Ventures
Date Established	2014
Parent HQ & CV Locations	Parent: Munich, Germany Munich Re Ventures: San Francisco (HQ) and London
Charter	Corporate venturing activities that deliver both strategic and financial value through minority investments, business partnerships, and acquisitions. Mission to grow parent business by leveraging new technology-enabled products, services, and data to serve customers as well as to identify emergent insurance gaps in the start-up ecosystem.
Legal & Reporting Structure	• Separate legal entity housed within US-based Hartford Steam Boiler (CEO, SVP), led by externally recruited managing director Jacqueline LeSage Krause • Adapted Munich Re Ventures GP/LP structure forms innovative "CVC fund platform": Munich Re Ventures is GP in each of 3 separate funds, each fund has a single LP/specific Munich Re business entity (HSB, Munich Re, ERGO) • Separate portfolio strategies and investment committees have been created for each of the 3 funds (HSB, Munich Re, ERGO). IC structure: Munich Re Ventures MD + CEO of each entity + 2–4 other senior executives
CV Program Elements	• Investing (CVC) + Portfolio Management • Strategy and strategic investment themes • CVBD/Partnerships for BUs • M&A front end

Team Size	Currently 12 team members across three areas, with open roles to reach 20+ in total team in 2019 1. CVC–Investment professionals at all levels (external recruits) 2. Operations–VP +team coordinator (external recruits) 3. Portfolio Development–VP portfolio manager + junior strategy (external) + 2 strategic partnership development (1 internal seconded from each of ERGO and HSB)
Focus Areas	• InsurTech • AI and analytics • Industrial IoT • Mobility/autonomous vehicles • Digital health • Cybersecurity
Program Scale	• 20 investments, across spectrum of rounds • 10–12 new investments/year
Recent Sample Investments	• Fraugster • Hippo • Mnubo • Ridecell • Team8 • Zeguro
Selected Syndicate Partners	• VC: Aquiline, Anthemis, Bessemer Ventures, Earlybird Venture Capital, Felicis Ventures, GV, Kleiner Perkins, Oak HC/FT, Ribbit Capital, RPM Ventures, • CVC: BMWi, Comcast Ventures, CommerzVentures, Softbank, Sompo, Veronorte, XL Innovate

Description of Program Development Journey and Key Learnings

In late 2014, Hartford Steam Boiler, a subsidiary of global insurance giant Munich Re, established a corporate venturing program and recruited experienced CV executive Jacqueline LeSage Krause to build and lead the group. Previously VP of innovation and CVC at insurer Hartford Financial Services Group, LeSage Krause had built Hartford Ventures and led venture investing and alliances as well as internal innovation and incubation activities.

Munich Re / HSB Ventures launched with the Hartford Steam Boiler (HSB) unit, which now drives commercial and industrial IoT strategy for Munich Re. The new CV team was tasked with providing input to strategy direction as well as contributing to the building of IoT-enabled business, with the tools of what LeSage Krause calls "transactional innovation," including investments, partnerships, and M&A. Staffed with experienced, externally recruited CV specialists, the team hit the ground running, making successful investments such as IoT start-up relayr.

With the early success of the program with HSB, two other group divisions (Munich Re's Reinsurance Group and ERGO) expressed interest in expanding the program to include them. In response, and in order to enable delivery of customized program strategies and outcomes tuned to the needs of each of the three groups, LeSage Krause uniquely adapted the GP/LP fund structure so familiar in the venture capital world to suit the circumstances and requirements of corporate venturing and Munich Re. The result: the newly named Munich Re Ventures is GP in three individual captive funds: each business is the sole LP in its own fund with its own investment committee structure. LeSage Krause's vision for a corporate venturing "Fund Platform" is now a cornerstone of Munich Re Ventures' program, designed to enable each of its business partner/LPs with a customizable fund and a "buffet" of signature end-to-end CV&I capabilities (CVC investment, strategy, partnering, and M&A prep), and addressing priority innovation themes such as Industrial IoT, InsurTech, and AI for insurance. As Munich Re Ventures expands and scales, its innovative Fund Platform can be extended to include other types of funds, as well (e.g., for more Munich Re businesses, individually or as a group; for creation or participation in specialty funds focused on emerging tech or market; or for a hybrid fund including complementary external partners like other corporates, VCs, or geo-specific business partners).

Through deep and expanding internal business relationships, as well as leveraging team CVC expertise to play active roles in leading rounds, the Munich Re Ventures team is well-positioned to amplify the strategic value for portfolio companies and for Munich Re businesses.

Learning through market experience and collaborating with each business to address their strategic priorities, the seasoned CV team continues to expand activities geographically (offices in San Francisco and London, with plans for China and India) and to add tools/enhanced capabilities (e.g., warrants, ICOs) to the Munich Re Ventures Platform.

Key Program Design Elements

- **CV Platform for transactional innovation**
  Munich Re Ventures has adapted the traditional venture capital GP/LP model to create a unique CV platform (fund plus buffet of CV&I service offerings) designed to enable the team to offer each Munich Re business a customized end-to-end specialty investing fund appropriate to their strategic interest areas and innovation adoption timelines. Each fund has its own lean investment committee (IC), which includes the Munich Re Ventures MD, and three to five senior executives of the business unit, often including the CEO.
- **Wiring of parent business relationships**
  To ensure that both Munich Re Ventures and each Munich Re business partner are aligned and prepared to get the most out of their CV Funds, the Munich Re Ventures team has developed a structured approach to defining strategic investment themes and onboarding a new business owner. Each business agrees to an anticipated rate and pace of investment activity and types of partnerships, and a defined CV process, with sponsor and operational roles clear and resourced. The new business owner team is "onboarded" with VC 101 training and Munich Re Ventures' perspective on quality deal sourcing and innovation partnering with relevant start-ups.

- **Blended specialist CV team**

  The Munich Re Ventures team is a blend of externally recruited professionals, with all of the investment team having previous C/VC experience, and internal personnel with depth of knowledge of the LP business (ensures outside-in mapping and pathways to commercial landings). Risk and regulatory functions are leveraged from the group and business-specific functions. Reflecting the insight Munich Re Ventures can provide in emerging market/tech development, the investment team is heavily drawn from other CVCs, with the expectation that they also bring the necessary strategic consulting expertise to be able to advise and engage effectively with the BUs.

Best Example of How Business Model Works: relayr

IoT strategy => source => invest => partner => acquire

Portfolio company relayr demonstrates how the Munich Re Ventures model marries strategic value and investment, although acquisition of portfolio companies is not an overall goal of Munich Re Ventures' activities. HSB drives the commercial and industrial IoT strategy for Munich Re. The early strategic corporate venturing activities were only in HSB, and the investment team was highly involved in development of the IoT strategy and building of the business via transactional innovation, including investments, partnerships, and M&A. Munich Re Ventures met relayr in late 2015 through multiple people in their network and facilitated an early pilot with HSB. Munich Re Ventures then led the company's Series B round, in which Deutsche Telecom participated, along with new and existing investors. This was the fourth IoT venture investment in the Munich Re Ventures portfolio. Along with the investment, Munich Re Ventures helped craft a significant partnership with relayr for bringing a new-to-the-world type of insurance product to the market, creating a unique selling proposition for relayr and opening up a new market for HSB and Munich Re at the same time. Over time, as relayr and HSB evolved their separate strategies within the emergent IoT space, their strategic relevance to each other increased, ultimately resulting in the acquisition of relayr by HSB/Munich Re in October of 2018 for $300 million.

Perspective: Top Three Things Deemed Essential to Munich Re Ventures' Development and Scale

1. **Agile, adaptable, and extensible CV and Fund Platform model**

   Munich Re Ventures has built the structural foundation to make it easy to fire up additional funds and LPs. For operating efficiency, the team is not distributed or allocated to specific funds (but rather to investment spaces and geographies)—and operates like one fund via team and processes. Within the funds, Munich Re Ventures has flexibility in the kinds of deals it will pursue, including both direct and LP investments and warrants. Fund differentiation comes with the approach to individual investment themes and commercial landing strategies.

   The CV Platform offers the potential to support more entities and create variations on the current Munich Re Ventures GP/LP model. For example, a specialty fund focused on an emerging tech or market arena, or a hybrid model that might cross-pollinate internal business group LPs with external CV or VC entities as LPs.

2. **Commitment to CV institutionalization**

   From even the early days as the strategic corporate venturing unit of HSB, Munich Re Ventures operations have been designed for repeatability, predictability, and scalability. The team has developed standard processes and templates for most key CV activities including:
   - Strategic theme development (collaborative approach with BUs)
   - Fund business partner onboarding
   - Strategic partnering (relationship development and management)
   - Performance reporting (quarterly reports)

3. **Team retention and recruitment**

   The Munich Re Ventures program's uniqueness and visibility have enabled the recruitment of capable senior professional team members. However, talent retention and team expansion at the right pace will be critical to meet program value delivery and scalability goals. And with Munich Re Ventures leading rounds/taking board seats across all funds, the current team is likely to face band-width issues.

The next phase of Munich Re Ventures program development will likely need to include HR strategy adaptations (for CV-specific levels, compensation, career paths, succession planning) to ensure competitiveness in the battle for top talent.

How Is Munich Re Ventures Measured?

Like most CV programs, Munich Re Ventures reports on both financial performance and strategic value at both the fund and aggregate platform levels. For each strategic theme and portfolio company, this includes information on the theme, BU owner, business goal, and progress along strategic framework.

CHAPTER 5

Resiliency Phase (Years 7–9+)

The Goal: Demonstrate long-term CV program resiliency in the face of constant change: external markets, business models, technologies; internal corporate strategic shifts, business downturns, and executive transitions.

("No complacency")

What's Happening:

- **Focus**: Broadened CV program charter/mandate to address new sectors and larger "market-maker" opportunities, priority geographic (global) expansion
- **Operating style**: CV Platform optimized for scale and adaptability: team structure and processes to support large scale CVC investing along with the networked CVBD resources to drive impactful portfolio/parent/ecosystem collaborations
- **Performance**: Numerous significant portfolio wins, buttressed by sophisticated portfolio management function and infrastructure to track/report on clear CV program success metrics, lead to parent and external approbation

The Challenge: *How to stay relevant and agile through environmental "oscillations" without damaging the CV program brand and position inside and outside, and especially without disenfranchising portfolio companies?*

Executive Summary

CV programs still active after seven to nine years have entrenched themselves as an essential corporate innovation function, contributing significant strategic insight and value along with financial self-sufficiency. However, there can be no complacency, even for programs with long strategic investing history, large portfolios, and strong performance track records, as they are guaranteed to face constant changes in external markets, business models, and technologies, as well as internal corporate strategic shifts, business downturns, and executive transitions.

Program continuity and scalability are enabled by the ability to adapt institutionalized teams, programs, and incentives over time, and to manage changes in parent strategy and leadership without undermining professional venture investing and value delivery credibility on the outside.

High-Performer Hallmarks

1. **CV program strategic role and continuous influence on parent growth and innovation strategy well-established**, often supplemented by the ability to make bigger bets (e.g., growth PE, M&A) and offer multipath options for start-up collaborations (partner, invest, co-develop, license, etc.)

2. **Optimized CV program platform**: Purpose-built end-to-end investing processes with fully staffed CVC and CVBD functions led by senior peers and supported by robust portfolio management function

3. **Savvy community management/strategic communications capabilities** (inside-out, outside-in) play essential role in enhancing and leveraging CV program leadership positioning and value to all stakeholders (corporate parent, CV team, start-ups, ecosystem partners)

High-performing programs bring exceptional understanding of their corporate parents' core businesses, operations, organization, and culture and are agile and creative in adapting investment strategy and structure to changing internal and external circumstances while maintaining corporate relevance and strategic alignment. The CV leader may occupy a seat at the executive table in parent transformational discussions (e.g., Wendell Brooks, SVP Intel Corp and president Intel Capital; Sue Siegel, GE Chief Innovation Officer and CEO, GE Ventures

Key enablers of an optimized CV program platform often include:

- Standard CV team specs within a specialized "CV track" (comp/titles/career path/succession planning)
- "CV partner-driven" investment decision-making with light touch parent executive oversight
- Sophisticated strategic portfolio and performance management team supported by custom tracking and reporting systems
- Communications strategy = business strategy for successful programs which understand how to amplify CV program leadership positioning and drive value for all key stakeholder communities

Threats and Antibodies

The larger, more successful, and more mature the CV program, the more challenging to be agile in weathering parental down cycles/changes in industry position, and or shifts in strategies and core priorities that lead to organizational overhauls.

Frequent challenges include:

- **The portfolio pivot**

    The need to pivot portfolio strategy/goals and redirect sizeable program operations and teams can force CV leadership to "right size" the portfolio, seek earlier exits, and create portfolio company stewardship conflicts.

    Externally, the CV leadership and team face challenges in maintaining leadership positioning and trusted network while buffering that network and portfolio companies against internal slowdowns, new reporting structures, and so on.

    Internally, the CVBD team feels pressure to keep vital internal connections identified and committed and operating to ensure that the pace/quality of parent/portfolio company engagement and value delivery is maintained.

- **Keeping the team "in the socket"**

    Retention becomes the watchword for established "brand" programs, which are frequent recruiting targets for newer CVCs, as well as VCs and start-ups. Senior team members who have "maxed out" internally are highly desirable externally where there are greater opportunities for next-level leadership positions and richer compensation. (Per Thelander compensation research, CV programs source more than 50 percent of their teams from other CVCs or VC/PE firms.)

    The ante goes up to keep high-performance CVC and CVBD individuals and their personal "equity value" to the program on board to avoid loss of vital network connections, and external ecosystem intelligence/partners.

- **Funding the next round**

    CV leadership often faces increasing pressure to leverage earned program credibility for greater value: bigger minority investments, strategic amplifiers through PE/rollups, and more expansive business and portfolio partnering programs. The need for a higher level of funding can force hard discussions around diversifying risk/reducing vulnerability by including funding from external partners (multicorporate LPs) versus the desire to keep a highly strategic program internally controlled and wholly owned (parent as sole LP).

    Note: Wholesale changes like acquisition of parent or unit divestiture can effectively downgrade mature, successful programs or turn them into outright casualties.

Resiliency Phase Design Rules
Charter

1. **Constantly reassess CV program role and opportunities to guide parent innovation strategy and CV program optionality**

    Established CV programs survive and thrive by dint of their ability to continuously reassess and adapt their objectives, roles, and investment theses to maintain a direct connection with and significant contribution to corporate and BU innovation strategy—a "seat at the table."

They can offer expert views on emerging markets, technologies, and business models with sophisticated approaches for tracking and framing new, rapidly developing ecologies around business areas strategically important to the parent. And they are well positioned to drive shared CV program/parent accountability for ensuring portfolio company landing and strategic impact.

But critical to program longevity are agility and creativity in adapting to changing internal and external circumstances while maintaining corporate relevance and strategic alignment. This resiliency is essential when the parent faces changes that push large-scale strategic pivots/transformations.

2. **Define and align expanded corporate venturing tool kit**

High-performance CV programs at scale have well-established roles and influence on parent innovation strategy, with minority investing often supplemented by the ability to make bigger bets (e.g., PE, M&A) and/or to facilitate other complementary options for collaboration with start-ups (partner, license, co-develop) across different time horizons (see Figure 1):

- Roadmap input (Short term)
- Adjacency landscapes (medium term, make-buy-partner guidance)
- "Future of" reimagined, new business creation (long term)

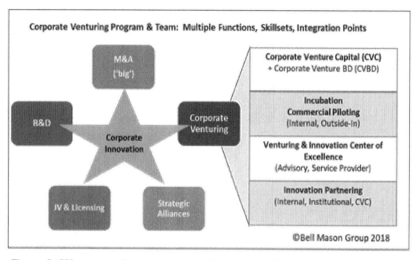

Figure 2: CV program & team: multiple functions, skill sets, integration points

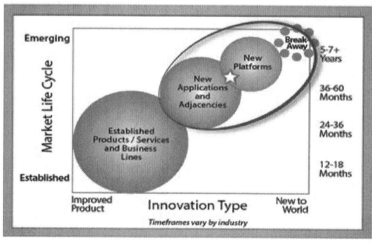

Figure 1: Spectrum of Innovation, and the "sweet spot" for leveraging CV know-how and optimizing parent company advantages (© Bell Mason Group 2011)

Increasingly these programs, headed by senior corporate executives, are prosecuting broader, more sophisticated investment theses with a range of tools/complementary functions/professional teams integrated in a higher-level innovation function.

For example, Wendell Brooks, president of Intel Capital and SVP of Intel Corporation, has responsibility for "strategic growth" driven by equity investing, M&A, alliances, and incubation. Vanessa Colella, president of Citi Ventures and chief innovation officer of Citigroup, oversees a program that integrates venture investing, incubation, labs, and innovation partnering.

3. **Prepare for seamless leadership transitions—Parent executive, CV program sponsor, CV head**

    Transitions are tests of CV program strategic relevance and ability to maintain external momentum. (Rule of thumb: enduring programs have survived at least three executive transitions or major strategic shifts.)

    Factors that improve likelihood of survival:

    - Program is seen as continuously significant strategic value contributor with an established role in parent innovation portfolio and an external reputation as a top-tier brand.
    - CV program and team structure, operations, governance, and reporting have been refined and institutionalized within the parent.
    - Standard process is in place for allocating investment funding or evergreen/self-funding where returns may be poured back into the CV program.
    - Effective succession planning/CV leadership transition management.

    In eight years marked by massive changes in health care and multiple Merck leadership changes, GHI's starting vision for Digital Health ("data as the currency") and its ecosystem approach to portfolio and partnering strategy has enabled the program to be consistently impactful and timely. (See Merck GHI Profile at the end of chapter 5.)

    And Intel Capital has consistently demonstrated the agility to morph its massive program to address four distinct eras for parent Intel under four very different leaders. (See Intel Capital Profile at the end of Chapter 5.)

Process

4. **Optimize end-to-end CV platform for scale, agility, and adaptability**
   Team structure and processes are institutionalized to support agile, large-scale CVC investing along with the aligned CVBD infrastructure to manage pilots and parent/ecosystem business collaborations.
   Key capabilities include:
   - Marketing/strategic communications and ecosystem relationship management engine
   - Fully integrated/overlapping CVC and CVBD teams, pipelines, and processes
   - Parent-side champions and "catchers" wired to obtain maximum value from portfolio collaborations

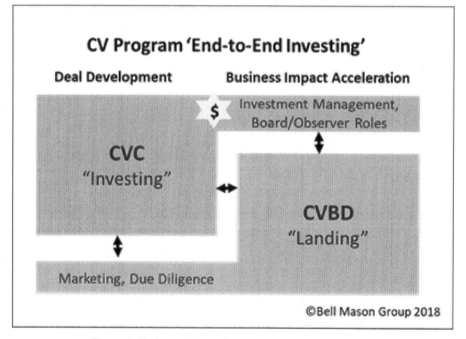

Figure 3: End-to-end investing (sourcing to landing spot)

- Robust portfolio management function and systems to capture and communicate program/portfolio value

5. **Extend program governance from investment decision-making to landing accountability**

As a reflection of parent respect for CV team investment expertise and track record, investment committee (IC) structures and processes have evolved to allow lean, or even autonomous CV team decision-making (e.g., VC partner model) as in the case of Intel Capital.

At the same time, an end-to-end focus ensures that investment decisions reflect CVBD/parent perspectives on investee company quality/potential value, while CVC investors play an ongoing role in portfolio strategic value delivery.

For the Merck GHI portfolio, IC members have accountability for ensuring parent/portfolio engagement as well as for making investment decisions. And Citi Ventures investment team performance metrics include ability to drive commercialization.

Team

6. **Partner with parent HR to create differentiated "CV track," maintain externally competitive compensation packages**

CV program scale, longevity, and strong track record can bring unique advantages:
- Attractive brand for CV team recruitment
- Low leadership attrition rate
  - o Intel Capital average MD tenure: fifteen years
  - o Citi Ventures Investment MD tenure: eight years, no defections
  - o Merck GHI MD tenure: eight years, no defections
- Increased leverage with parent HR to drive development of specialized "CV track"
  - o Standard CV team specs
  - o Exceptional compensation structures (CVC and CVBD)

    o   Titles/banding (externally/internally aligned)
- Career paths with professional development curriculum
- Succession planning

Q&A with Mark Radcliffe/DLA Piper: Why do you recommend that quali-fied members of the corporate venture investing team rather than BU or functional representatives of the parent hold the board seats or observer roles?

Mark Radcliffe: Corporate venture capitalists have issues different from traditional financial investors: (1) the control of the use of confidential information for portfolio companies is quite different from traditional financial investors, and (2) the increased number of corporate venture capitalists taking board seats require understanding of the responsibilities and expectations of the company and other board members. Start-ups tend to be very concerned that information provided to the corporate venture investors will be provided to business units and used to develop competing products or services.

    Corporate venture capitalists are taking seats on the board of directors on a more regular basis, but corporate venture capitalists need to under-stand the requirements of such membership and the expectations of the start-up and other investors for such participation. The person serving on a board of directors undertakes two fiduciary duties owed to all of the cor-poration's stockholders: (1) the duty of care, and (2) the duty of loyalty. The duty of loyalty also includes subsidiary duties of confidentiality and duty of disclosure (to stockholders). These obligations are personal to the indi-vidual and can result in personal liability for the individual if these duties are violated. However, board members can substantially reduce their potential liability by ensuring that their actions meet the standards of the "business judgment" rule.

    The individuals taking those positions will have high visibility to the start-up and the other investors and will have a significant effect on the reputation of the corporate venture capital investor. They need to understand their duties and the expectations of other board members.

For example, the material provided at the board meeting will frequently include the start-up's most sensitive information, and individuals serving as board members must be very careful in its disclosure and use within the parent organization. Given these obligations, it is very important that these individuals be part of the CVC organization and not from a business unit and that they be appropriately trained. We have seen even the most senior executives of parent organizations misunderstand these roles and believe that board information should be widely shared within the parent organization. Experienced outside counsel can assist in training the prospective board members as well as educating executives at the parent organizations about these limits. Prospective board members also need to understand the culture of the particular board that they are joining: for example, is it dominated by a single board member or are the board members relatively equal? We strongly recommend that they develop personal relationships with the other board members to enable them to be a "trusted" party if the board needs to make tough decisions. They also need to understand the venture ecosystem so that they can advise on funding options. We recommend that prospective board members be trained in the legal framework and best practices in serving on boards.

As the ante goes up to keep high-performance CVC and CVBD individuals and their personal equity value on board, top CV programs are partnering with informed HR leaders to develop/maintain culturally sensitive but competitive offers relative to other CVCs, VCs, and private companies.

For example, Citi HR leadership has recognized that Citi Ventures is a unique operation and has worked closely with the Ventures team to craft differentiated CV job descriptions/titles/bands and compensation approaches. And Intel Capital has been a leader in developing a specialist CV track, including standard CV roles/titles, formal professional development curricula, an entry-level "grow from within" program, and novel approaches for recognizing/rewarding portfolio financial performance.

7. **Plan for expansion of board member/observer pool**

As sophisticated CV programs increasingly lead rounds and want to play influential roles in guiding the development of portfolio

---

Q&A with Intel Capital: As corporates such as Intel Capital become more active in portfolio company development and value delivery, the role of CV team portfolio company board members/observers becomes more critical. Given the scale of the Intel Capital portfolio, what steps are taken to develop a large enough pool of qualified board members/observers among the senior CV team and to prepare them to manage potential risks/conflicts?

Nick Washburn/Intel Capital COO: Intel Capital takes our roles as a director or observer on the boards of portfolio companies very seriously. Our investment professionals have a great deal of experience individually and collectively, plus access to a shared body of knowledge honed over time from experience in over 1,500 investments and over 650 successful exits.

We have developed an annual training curriculum for all members of our investment organization, in conjunction with our extremely knowledgeable legal team, that leverages years of learnings. This curriculum is updated for the latest legal developments, focusing on managing conflicts of interest and, for directors, fiduciary duties. Beyond the legal requirements and practices of good governance, we focus on being engaged in ways that add value, with the investor playing an important role in working directly with the portfolio company executives and other board members, and with experts from across Intel.

On a more informal basis, our team conducts monthly group syncs that involve a variety of trainings and learning pass-downs, which often include practical ways to add value as a director or observer. We share case studies and best practices within the team, learning from the circumstances that led to impairments or the strategies that led to better outcomes at each stage of a start-up's growth and to an eventual exit.

> We limit the total number of director and observer roles our investors can have at a given time, to ensure attention is devoted to helping our portfolio companies in these important roles. As an investor leading rounds, we are focused on adding value to our portfolio companies, and this includes being an active director or observer. Knowledge sharing and proper training, both formal and informal, and guidelines help us deliver on this mandate.

companies, more teams are faced with the need for qualified senior investment professionals who understand how to be responsible board members/observers while representing the interests of the corporate parent.

For those programs whose portfolio growth is outstripping their team's capacity, this can force senior team members to exceed the recommended three to five seats per person, increasing risks and raising opportunity costs on their time.

Large-scale programs have developed a CV professional board/observer qualification approaches that typically include:

- Corporate board/observer training curriculum
- On-the-job shadowing before soloing
- Seasoning in the parent's corporate culture and environment

As a rule of thumb, lead time to "seasoning" is a minimum of one year as even experienced externally recruited investors/board members need to demonstrate competency that validates their skill and ensures corporate parent fluency to reduce corporate risk/exposure.

Innovation Partnering

8. **Formalize/institutionalize parent BU and functional partnerships**
   Through experience and track records, established CV programs are taking BU/strategic focus area partnerships to the next level, some with formal working agreements that specify the following:

- Collaborative investment strategy development and committed funding
- Market insight delivery and quarterly/annual portfolio introduction targets
- Education of internal customers/partners re: curating for right-fit solutions
- Designated venture development support funds, ownership, and roles along the integrated pipeline from investment to commercialization
- Parent-side "wiring" to obtain maximum value from collaborations (accountable sponsors, SMEs and "catchers," hand-off processes, PMO, flex resourcing, value capture tracking, etc.)

9. **Leverage ability to create higher-level market development theses and CV program reputation to expand network reach and curate for impactful ecosystem partnerships**

Enduring programs excel at framing emerging markets/technologies and ecosystems and are well positioned to attract and add value to compelling start-ups, co-investors, and partners.

Merck GHI's Digital Health ecosystem vision enables start-ups to self-identify and illustrates to potential partners the team's depth of emerging market insight and expertise.

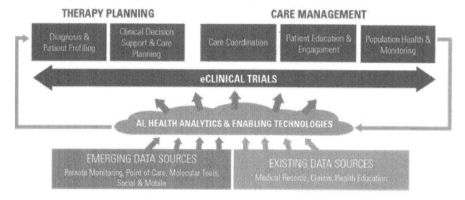

Figure 4: © Merck Global Health Innovation Fund—Ecosystem vision for portfolio and partnering strategy (Source: GHI website)

At the same time, a well-established reputation for consistent "good investing behavior" and program quality lays the foundation for the development of sophisticated innovation partnering programs:

- Deep networks and portfolio partnerships with top institutional investors (e.g., Citi Ventures/Andreessen Horowitz)
- Complementary CVC ecosystem development partnerships and multi-VC syndicates (e.g., Intel Capital value multiplier program)
- Ongoing commitment to the best interests of the portfolio, even when the priorities of the Parent and investee companies may diverge

Q&A with Intel Capital: How does Intel Capital walk the tightrope between supporting the best interests of its large portfolio of investments ("good investor behavior") while staying "in phase" with the parent company's shifts in business strategies and management changes?

Nick Washburn/Intel Capital COO: First and foremost, Intel Capital is a thesis-driven venture capital organization, where our investment theses are predicated on adding value to our portfolio companies. Intel Capital works relentlessly to enable our portfolio companies to scale and succeed, leveraging Intel's business unit expertise and other unique assets from across Intel. Additionally, all our investments must be financially attractive, as we seek to maximize financial returns to Intel and its shareholders.

While some corporate venture organizations may invest only in proven technology or companies aligned to their current business unit strategies, we tend to apply a broader lens and look for potentially disruptive "pathfinding" start-ups. Our role is to invest with a view toward the future in companies that may create new markets or new capabilities. We define the areas where we invest, and we leverage the deep technical and business knowledge within Intel to collaborate with the companies in our portfolio. In an ideal world, Intel's experts work together with a start-up to solve problems or create new industry solutions, so there is a mutually beneficial alignment of interests and strategies. Yet, with emerging technologies and new markets, there is often a level of risk and uncertainty for the start-up and for the parent company. Some "pathfinding" start-ups end up "pivoting" in a different direction, making them less strategically relevant for Intel. And even large companies like Intel reprioritize strategies, at times creating or exiting entire businesses, which can result in portfolio companies with limited strategic engagement.

Management changes are a fact of life in modern corporations, and Intel is no exception. Intel Capital strives to cultivate broad and deep relationships between a portfolio company and multiple contacts within Intel. This decreases the dependency on any one individual manager as an advocate for a portfolio company. As a portfolio company evolves, it may benefit from engaging with variety of Intel experts, including engineers, sales, marketing, and senior business unit general managers, or other specialized experts.

When business units at Intel undergo management or strategy changes that result in investments becoming less strategically relevant to Intel, we continue to focus on adding value to our portfolio companies to drive top-line growth, as this will naturally drive venture returns for Intel. This is the benefit of investing in both financially attractive and strategically relevant companies—as strategy shifts, the financial profile can continue to deliver returns to Intel. Ultimately, we strive to have transparent relationships with both our portfolio companies and business unit colleagues, as mutual trust, respect, and hard work ensure there is accretion of value to all our "customers"—be they the founders we partner with or Intel itself.

Performance

10. **Tune portfolio management and reporting framework and processes for adjustability**

    A hallmark of a high-performance team and an enduring program is consistency in meeting strategic and financial goals, while adjusting for alignment with corporate strategy and organizational shifts. By this point, established programs have strategic portfolio tracking and reporting managed by a dedicated professional team who have developed performance scorecards that reflect corporate language/culture and employ streamlined processes and software.

    Scorecards typically integrate such elements as the following:
    - **Financial performance metrics**: Investment quality indicators
      o Top-quartile VC IRR, cash-on-cash
      o Portfolio value
      o "Evergreen" status—progress toward being self-funding
    - **Strategic impact metrics**: Parent business impact indicators
      o Categories (related to program charter/objectives)
      o Quantification (e.g., time, money [revenues and savings], new customers, new markets, risk reduction, etc.)
    - **Operational metrics**: Program quality and effectiveness indicators
      o End-to-end investing waterfall/pipeline (e.g., sourcing, percentage of portfolio moving from investment through to commercialization)
      o PR/thought leadership (key internal/external events, publications, brand recognition/awards, portfolio company success stories)

11. **Set and communicate clear program success metrics highlighting contributions to parent, portfolio and partners**

    Communications strategy equals business strategy for successful programs that understand how to articulate CV program objectives, amplify program leadership positioning, and illustrate value for all key stakeholder communities (corporate parent, CV team, start-ups, ecosystem partners)

Savvy community management/strategic communications capabilities (inside-out, outside-in) play an essential role in

- delivering outside-in corporate education/insights, an increasingly significant part of the CV charter given the speed of new technology commercialization and emerging market development;
- validating trust and respect among external ecosystem players/partners and serving as a vital enabler of successful stakeholder collaborations, partnering, and end-to-end investing;
- highlighting potential CV program value to start-ups.

Intel Capital and Citi Ventures both excel at crystallizing key messages to articulate program objectives and quality. (See figures 5 and 6.)

Intel Capital–Corporate Transformation Focus (Chip Company to Data Company)

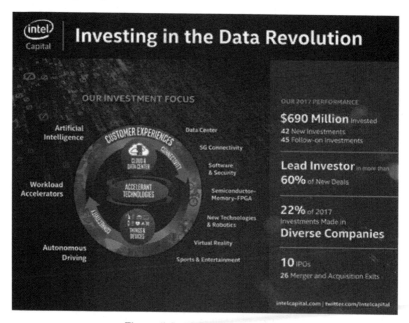

Figure 5: Intel Capital scorecard

Citi Ventures–Innovation Commercialization Focus

citi VENTURES "We Bring the Outside In: To gain proprietary, early access to relevant insights that can help start-up founders scale their businesses"

Citi Ventures: Venture Investing at a Glance	
Ecosystem meetings across 5 focus areas 1. Financial services and technology 2. Data analytics and machine learning 3. Commerce and payments 4. Security and enterprise IT 5. Customer experience and marketing	1,000 meetings/year
Start-ups introduced to Citi each year	> 50
Active portfolio companies	>40
Portfolio companies commercialized within Citi	60% of portfolio

Figure 6: Citi Ventures venture investing at a glance

RESILIENCY PHASE DESIGN RULES

Charter	1. Constantly re-assess CV program role and opportunities to guide parent innovation strategy and CV program optionality 2. Define & align expanded corporate venturing toolkit 3. Prepare for seamless leadership transitions
Process	4. Optimize end-to-end CV platform for scale, agility and adaptability 5. Extend program governance from investment decision making to landing accountability
Team	6. Partner with parent HR to create differentiated CV "track;" maintain externally competitive CV compensation packages 7. Plan for expansion of board member/observer pool
Innovation Partnering	8. Formalize/institutionalize parent BU and functional partnerships 9. Leverage ability to create higher level market development theses and CV program reputation to expand network reach and curate for impactful ecosystem partnerships
Performance	10. Tune portfolio management and reporting framework and processes for adjustability 11. Set and communicate clear program success metrics highlighting contributions to parent, portfolio and partners

HIGH PERFORMER PROFILES
Resiliency Phase (Years 7–9+)
PROGRAM PROFILE: CITI VENTURES

Program Name	Citi Ventures
Date Established	2006
Parent HQ & CV Locations	Parent HQ: New York, NY Citi Ventures: San Francisco (HQ); Palo Alto, CA; New York; Israel; London
Charter	Citi Ventures is the innovation engine of Citi, committed to conceiving, launching, and scaling new initiatives with the potential to transform the future of financial services. We accelerate innovation at Citi by investing in start-ups, piloting new technologies, and testing new solutions and business models through our Citi Innovation Labs and Citi Businesses.
Legal, Reporting Structure	• Dedicated unit/team within Citi • Headed by Citi's chief innovation officer, Vanessa Colella • Reports to CFO (John Gerspach)
CV Program Elements	• CVC (Invest) • D10X (Incubate) • Innovation Network/Emerging Technology (Explore) • Ventures Studio (Accelerate)
Team Size	• Venture Investing (Invest)–12 • D10X (Accelerate)–14 • Innovation NW/Emerging Tech (Labs)–2 • Ventures Studio–7 EIRs
Focus Areas	• Financial services and tech • Data analytics and machine learning • Commerce and payments • Security and enterprise IT • Customer experience and marketing

Program Scale	• 50 active investments (65 historical) • 13 exits (per Crunchbase) • 8–10 annual new investments
Sample Investments	• Recent: Freebird, Hopper, Ondot • Exits: Square, Jet, DocuSign, Silver Tail
Select Syndicate Partners	• CVC: Amex, Capital One, Cisco, GV, Intel Capital, Microsoft • VC: Andreesen Horowitz, Battery, DFJ, Khosla, KP, Menlo, NEA

Description of Program Development Journey

Corporate venturing at Citi started in 2006 with the establishment of Citi Growth Ventures to focus on consumer innovations, beginning with transformational core business projects (e.g., next-gen transit and retail spaces), incubated spinouts, and a small number of minority investments. The program survived the 2008 financial collapse and was funded to go forward.

By 2008, the Citi Ventures program was expanded and formalized under the newly appointed first Citi Chief Innovation Officer, Debby Hopkins, who envisioned an interconnected innovation model:

- Establishment of dedicated functional innovation teams (outside-in and inside-out): Venture Investing (CVC), Incubation (D10X), Innovation Network
- Relocation of Citi Ventures HQ to Silicon Valley (2010), and expansion of global program footprint (Asia-Pacific, Europe)
- Recruitment of professional VC investors/Silicon Valley veterans and venturing, innovation, and technology specialists who brought strong networks and venture development experience (e.g., Arvind Purushotham/Menlo Ventures; Vanessa Colella/Citi, USVP, Yahoo)

During this period, Citi Ventures delivered multiple high-profile wins with program value recognized both inside and outside Citi.

Citi Ventures today is recognized as a top-tier CV program and partner. The CIO/Citi Ventures leadership reins were seamlessly transitioned to Citi senior executive and Citi Ventures veteran Vanessa Colella in 2016. She now oversees four complementary venturing and innovation teams.

1. **Venture Investing (Invest)**

    The VI team sources, exercises due diligence, and invests in leading-edge start-ups in financial services. Leveraging internal networks, external ecosystem relationships, and meetings with more than a thousand start-ups per year, the VI team develops a deep understanding of emerging technologies, applications, business models, and industry trends to crystallize investment themes. They then identify distinctive start-ups to watch, invest in, and facilitate commercialization with through proof of concepts, pilots, and contracts signed with Citi and/or Citi's clients.

2. **D10X (Incubate)**

Grounded in principles of venture capital and the Lean Start-Up methodology, D10X provides Citi employees with the opportunity to create and test new solutions that are at least ten times better for clients. Since 2016, over 1,500 employees have participated in the program with more than 200 of them working on more than 100 internal start-up ideas in 2018 (e.g., Proxymity, a proxy voting platform directly connecting and authenticating issuers with investors while making shareholder voting more efficient, accurate, and transparent).

3. **Ventures Studio (Accelerate)**

Ventures Studio focuses on enabling multiparty solutions that drive economic vitality for people, businesses, and cities with the belief that broad-based growth requires like-minded partners to come together to address the biggest challenges. For example, Citi Ventures created the Citi University Partnerships in Innovation and Discovery (CUPID) program to engage and embed students from leading universities in innovation efforts across Citi.

4. **Innovation Network (Explore)**

Through the Innovation Network, Citi Ventures researches emerging technology trends and business applications by leveraging work in the innovation ecosystem. The team looks at transformational technologies like augmented reality, blockchain for digital identity, and 5G-powered IoT and edge computing.

Key Program Design Elements

- **Financial services innovation vision (insights for Citi, partners, portfolio)**

  Citi Ventures is uniquely structured to develop a financial services innovation vision and ecosystem perspective that combines the domain expertise/market leadership/resources of Citi businesses with future-focused external market insights and relationships provided through the Venture Investing and Innovation Network teams.

This enables the CV team to bring the outside into Citi, informing business leaders of emerging technology, business models, and growth patterns in the start-up landscape as well as making introductions to leading ventures with enterprise-ready technology and new business models. And the VI team provides valuable external venture context for internal innovation initiatives driven by the D10X team.

- **Commitment to parent commercial engagement (differentiation as investor)**

  Post any investment, the CV team works to accelerate and scale each start-up's growth through partnership with the larger Citi organization. More than 60 percent of the Citi Ventures investment portfolio have conducted a pilot with Citi or are fully commercialized. To accomplish this, the CV team is tightly connected to Citi's businesses, both strategically and operationally, with investors incented for successful commercial collaborations:

  o   20 percent of VI team time is spent with Citi leadership and key operational personnel to understand priorities/road map/interests and discuss implications of trends (e.g., machine learning).

  o   Catalyst program (four to five years old, seven to eight people)—BUs second/embed high performers/BD professionals to work with portfolio companies and act as a bridge between Citi Ventures and Citi businesses. Helps to bring outside innovation and venturing thinking in to Bus.

  o   Investment team commercialization incentives: investment team performance metrics include ability to drive commercialization (measured and tracked via detailed pipeline with stages and tracking).

- **The Citi Ventures platform—business model and delivery "engine" for strategic/financial impact**

  Since 2006 and in the face of constant contextual changes, the Citi Ventures' expert multifunction team has consistently demonstrated agility and measurable value as a strategic innovation catalyst for Citi. And it has built a strong external reputation for program quality, professionalism, and ecosystem influence, with the ability to predictably deliver partner/portfolio company value-add. This has enabled the Citi Ventures program to survive and thrive through significant global economic events, multiple parent management reorganizations and changes of leadership, and shifts in Citi business priorities and strategies.

Citi's chief innovation officer, Vanessa Colella, has continued to nurture the blend of senior-level, externally recruited investment and innovation specialists who have broad external ecosystem networks with internally sourced team members who bring Citi infrastructure/network access and deep experience working within the corporate parent. The program operates with streamlined, institutionalized processes that provide considerable autonomy to key team members—e.g., the CVC leadership team has investment discretion and uses structured, standard due diligence and approval processes that enable transparency with potential portfolio companies. And along with the investment pipeline comes an overlapping Citi BU/function engagement pipeline that tracks progress toward commercialization and impact.

Best Example of How Business Model Works: HighRadius

Citi invested in and partnered with leading start-up HighRadius to use automation and artificial intelligence to bridge the gap between accounts payable and accounts receivable in B2B payments.

Traditionally, accounts payable and accounts receivable have been separate processes, but by using technology to move toward automation, companies can integrate them in a more streamlined, unified way. Given that Citi operates in ninety countries and has the largest receivables business in global banking, a partnership with HighRadius helps solve a major client pain point.

In July 2018, Citi's Treasury and Trade Solutions and High Radius announced Citi® Smart Match. Leveraging HighRadius's proprietary artificial intelligence (AI) and machine learning (ML) technology along with its own proprietary assets, Citi dramatically increases the efficiency and automation of the cash application process of matching open invoices to payments received for its corporate clients.

The partnership followed Citi Ventures investment in HighRadius in February 2018 and has produced bilateral benefits: Citi has learned how to use smart data tech to advantage clients, and the HighRadius product roadmap reflects the insight of a financial service market leader. Furthermore, HighRadius, tapping Citi's global distribution network, has closed numerous joint customers as part of an integrated solution with Citi.

Perspective: Top Three Things Deemed Essential to Citi Ventures Program's Scale and Longevity

1. **Expertise and access**

   Citi BU's/functions become even more open to Citi Ventures' perspective from the frontline of emerging markets, technologies and business models. And the CV team continues to develop their ability to contribute deep domain expertise, insights, and Citi access to actively inform portfolio company product roadmaps and enable scale.

2. **High-performance team, transparent VC principles**

   Critical to the ability to participate in best deals/partnerships, Citi Ventures recognizes the importance of retaining an "A" team that has investment discretion and relies on structured and transparent due diligence and approval processes.

   The founding VI leadership team have been on board for eight years. Citi HR leadership has recognized that Citi Ventures is a unique operation and has worked closely with the Ventures team to craft differentiated CV job descriptions/titles/bands and compensation approaches.

3. **Citi parent engagement and support**

   The Citi Ventures team accelerates the adoption and commercialization of new technologies and business models through tight linkages with the Citi parent. This allows them to make introductions across Citi's global network of industry experts, partners, and long-standing customer relationships and guide start-ups/new internal ventures on the inner workings of Citi through a curated process, staying with them throughout the journey.

How Is Citi Ventures Measured?

Citi Ventures is committed to building a high-quality innovation portfolio that is financially successful, but that is also interesting strategically. The team tracks the following:

- Financial performance metrics:
  - o Strong IRR
  - o Thirteen exits
- Strategic performance metrics:

    With a laser focus on commercialization, Citi Ventures has facilitated parent relationships with 60 percent of the Venture Investing portfolio and can show that the portfolio provides significant value (experience, capabilities, risk reduction).

    The team is disciplined about working with BUs/functions to define the strategic rationale for and quantify the monetary value of commercial activity driven by a portfolio company (e.g., joint clients, net revenue impact, reduced business costs) as well as less measurable secondary effects.

- Knowledge transfer/cultural impact metrics:
  - o D10X: number of participating employees, current projects, project wins/impact
  - o Catalyst Program: number of BU secondees, number of pilots/ commercialization projects
  - o Tech/market insights to BUs, CEO Summit/Demo days in Silicon Valley

PROGRAM PROFILE: INTEL CAPITAL

Program Name	Intel Capital
Date Established	1991
Parent HQ & CV Locations	Parent HQ–Santa Clara, CA Intel Capital–California, China, Israel, London, and Berlin
Charter	Intel Capital is a thesis-driven venture capital organization that leverages domain expertise to
	• identify the most promising portfolio companies; • use expertise, unique assets of Intel to drive value for portfolio companies; • maximize financial returns to Intel and its shareholders.
Legal, Reporting Structure	• Division of Intel Corporation • Wendell Brooks, senior vice president, Intel Corp., and president, Intel Capital
CV Program Elements	• Corporate venture end-to-end investing • Portfolio development: portfolio business development, business unit relations, strategic events management, marketing, and PR • Portfolio tracking, analysis, reporting functions
Team Size (~80)	• President (also leads M&A, Emerging Growth Incubation Group, and Sports BU) • CVC/Investment team: Led by investment committee, COO and 4 senior managing directors. Global organization of approximately 40 experienced investors. • Portfolio development: Led by VP/MD, team of about 15 specialists delivering focused value to portfolio companies to optimize investment theses. Activities include internal BU alignment, connections with key experts, research, curated customer introductions, marketing and PR, staffing support, and other services to help accelerate portfolio company outcomes. • Investment support: legal, finance, portfolio analytics.

Focus Areas	Investing themes grouped around primary domains aligned with Intel Corporation's data-centric strategy: • Artificial intelligence (AI) • Autonomous and mobility management • Datacenter hardware, software, and cloud • Data and insights • Enabling technology • 5G, next-generation communications, datacenter networking and connectivity • Future silicon manufacturing technology and memory • Internet of things (IoT) • Next-generation compute/devices
Program Scale	• More than $12 billion invested in over 1,500 companies globally. • Over 650 exits (IPOs and acquisitions) • Annual investing rate: ~$350 million, ~ 30 new deals/year + follow-ons
Sample Investments	Intel Capital has made a number of well-known investments around the globe, including AVG, Broadcom, Carbon Black, CNET, Citrix Systems, Cloudera, Docusign, GoodData, Inktomi, Insyde Software, iZettle, Kingsoft, LogMeIn, Marvell, Mellanox, MongoDB, NetPosa, NIIT, PCCW, RedHat, Rediff.com, Switch, YuMe, Virtustream, VMware, and many more.
Sample Syndicate Partners	Intel Capital co-invests globally with leading VC and CVC firms that provide unique value to entrepreneurs. A recent sample: Andreesen Horowitz, Dell, Google Ventures, In-Q-Tel, Kleiner Perkins, M12 (Microsoft), New Enterprise Associates, Samsung.

Description of Program Development Journey and Key Learnings

From its establishment in 1991 as Corporate Business Development (CBD) to today, Intel Capital has always been the front-facing arm of Intel, pursuing innovation and growth. Intel Capital continues to be a leader in driving the evolution of CVC practices, professionalization, and value delivery. Over the last twenty-seven years, in the face of changes in technology and market shifts/disruptions and through multiple economic cycles, Intel Capital has been able to evolve organizationally, stay strategically relevant, and expand the program's influence. This agility and adaptability can be seen in Intel Capital's willingness to periodically adjust its structure, size, and focus areas in pursuit of the best transactions. Over time, there have been different approaches to the breadth of the investment field, the alignment with internal BUs, the compensation model, and portfolio development offerings. What has remained consistent is the commitment of Intel Corporation to fund more than $300 million annually for forward-sensing investments.

There have been four distinct phases/leaders in Intel Capital's development and evolution:

1. **The beginning**/Les Vadasz (1991–2003)

    Vadasz, the fourth employee of Intel, was already long renowned as a technical expert and highly respected as one of Intel's core executives when he established Corporate Business Development (CBD) with the support of then–Intel CEO Andy Grove and other senior executives. From the beginning, the organization had distinct capabilities in Business Development, M&A, and equity investing with a mandate to expand beyond the core businesses of Intel. Vadasz assembled a team of leaders and created the cultural underpinnings of the organization that was soon renamed Intel Capital. They innovated a unique approach to strategic investing, with a focus on investments that were both strategically impactful and financially attractive, and a requirement that all deals consist of value exchange beyond "money for a percentage of ownership." Under Vadasz's leadership, Intel's first formal CVC deal management, approval processes, and focus on portfolio management were developed.

They sourced and invested in US and international companies to help BUs develop markets, foster demand for products, and identify and nurture new technologies. Representative investments: Ariba, Audible, Broadcom, Citrix Systems, Elpida, Marvel Technology Group, Micron, Rambus, Redhat, Research in Motion (RIM), Sohu.com, Starmedia, Verisign, VLSI, and WebMD.

2. **Program step-up during dot-com bust**/John Miner (2003–2005)

Miner, whose background at Intel was BU management, took the helm and navigated Intel Capital through the bursting of the dot-com bubble, successfully balancing the need to conserve cash with the opportunity to double down for the future during an economic downturn. Some of those low-valuation investments ultimately became game changers for Intel. Learning through experience, Intel Capital evolved and formalized the minority investing process, recognizing the need to take meaningful stakes with follow-ons in order to be taken seriously by entrepreneurs and syndicate partners. With larger stakes, they increasingly took active board observer positions and appointed board directors. During this period, Intel Capital also expanded further abroad, correctly identifying major opportunities for the program in India and the Pacific Rim, and also enabling investments such as Sociedad Nacional de Procesamiento de Datos (SONDA) for market development in Latin America. Other investments in this era delivered new capabilities to the growing market for compute. Examples include AVG (antivirus security software for PCs), E-Ink (innovative screen technology), and Vocera (wearable, hands-free, voice-over IP communications targeted toward healthcare).

3. **Professionalization, the impact delivery engine, and scale**/ Arvind Sodhani (2005–2016)

Under Sodhani, formerly treasurer of Intel, Intel Capital moved to the next level in scale and the ability to deliver value to all stakeholders. During this time Intel Capital supported Intel's global strategies and sought the best innovations worldwide. At one point, investors were based in twenty-six countries, (supporting investments in fifty-seven countries), enabling deal-closer support to entrepreneurs and supporting Intel's global initiatives such as WiMax and investments to support the continued evolution of the PC and the growing businesses and technologies around mobile computing and data centers. Intel Capital achieved recognition as a global, tier 1 VC, known for both the quality of its investments and the operational support it provided through a robust portfolio development function. Recognizing the greatest needs of tech entrepreneurs, programs were established and staffed to connect portfolio companies with business unit experts and leaders and to develop portfolio business through curated customer introductions. In an effort to encourage retention of its high-performance team members, an innovative approach was developed to offer investment professionals upside incentives for successful exits—one of the first of its type in corporate venturing. Representative investments: Amplidata, ASML, Beceem, B-soft, Imagination, Inktome, iMall, iSteamplanet, Neusoft, Switch Communications, UQ Communications, and Virtustream.

4. **Intel corporate transformation/ Intel Capital program resiliency**/Wendell Brooks (2016–present)

The first Intel Capital leader to come from the outside, Brooks has a strong background in investment banking, M&A, and corporate development. He joined Intel to lead M&A and the Strategic Transactions Group in 2014 and was appointed president of Intel Capital in 2016. As of press time, he is responsible for all areas of inorganic strategic growth, including equity investing, M&A, and new business incubation.

In support of Intel's transformation from a "chip company to a data company," Brooks organized Intel Capital to play a more impactful role in expansion into new market segments, technology/business model explorations, and emerging ecosystem partnerships. Intel Capital continues to execute on this strategy, testing and refining the model for aligning and integrating equity investing with other growth tools, including M&A and emerging growth incubation.

Brooks refined Intel Capital's strategy to make fewer, bigger bets to increase the impact of investments in strategic domains. Intel Capital team members are taking more active roles (as board members, CVC and innovation partners, and in portfolio company development) to accelerate outcomes for portfolio companies.

Brooks has been an advocate for diversity and inclusion. Under his leadership, Intel Capital has expanded its focus for his team and their portfolio companies. Brooks is passionate about collaboration and has organized his leadership team to lead the investment committee and has empowered them by streamlining decision-making, encouraging debate, focusing on portfolio company outcomes, and aligning and rewarding team performance.

Key Program Design Elements

- **Future focused, thesis-driven investment strategy**

    Intel Capital focuses on investing for the future for Intel, in companies that create future trends, disruptive technologies, platforms, and newly forming or reshaping market segments that may be of strategic importance to Intel. Intel Capital defines its investment domains in advance, develops a thesis around how it can create value beyond investment dollars, and then actively pursues investments in these domains.

- **End-to-end investing model focusing on entrepreneurs**

    Intel Capital integrates a best-in-class global CVC investing team and process with a robust, institutionalized portfolio development and performance management function. Intel Capital is recognized as a Tier 1 VC investor, both by the scale/financial performance of the program and by the demonstrated operational value it contributes to portfolio company development.

- **Commitment to agility and adaptability**

    Intellectual rigor and use of data (combined with a bit of Andy Grove's famous paranoia) are hallmarks of Intel and Intel Capital. Metrics are established, and the internal and external signals are monitored. The organization adjusts and adapts continuously so investment and ecosystem partnering strategies, organizational structure, team recruitment/retention/development, and portfolio performance management are all relevant and aligned to support the charter.

Best Example of How Business Model Works: Virtustream

In 2009, Intel Capital actively tracked and engaged the emergence and growth of cloud computing and its potential use by enterprises, in addition to web-native companies. It identified Virtustream for its pioneering and somewhat contrarian approach to cloud computing: instead of building and deploying distributed web/mobile "stateless" apps, Virtustream built a cloud management platform that could run mission-critical, "stateful," latency-sensitive apps on a modern cloud architecture, on-premise or as a service—which had the potential to be particularly valuable to large enterprises.

Impressed by the Virtustream solution and its experienced team, Intel Capital invested in the Series A financing in early 2010 and even led subsequent financing rounds. The relationship between Intel and Virtustream flourished because of shared sales needs: Virtustream needed the credibility and reach of a large partner to gain access to large enterprises and their core applications, while Intel wanted a software solution provider to serve as a conduit through which to sell its new processing and security technology. The resulting relationship proved mutually beneficial: Virtustream received the technology, marketing, and sales support needed to gain access to large enterprise customers, as well as insight, advice, and board governance from experienced Intel Capital investment professionals, while Intel gained insight into the burgeoning cloud computing market segment and the market-leading solutions provider it wanted.

To help Virtustream scale, Intel Capital worked initially with the Intel sales and marketing team and, ultimately across Intel's Data Center Group to provide the needed introductions and technical credibility. The targeted introductions produced a material portion of Virtustream's revenues during the company's formative years, as well as a solid adoption of Intel's latest security offering at the time, known as TXT. Virtustream's CEO, Rodney Rogers, cited the initial traction from Intel customer referrals as a key to the company's early success.

In 2015, Virtustream was acquired by EMC for $1.2 billion, which not only created substantial investment returns for Intel Capital and the other investors, but further expanded Intel's opportunity to realize the strategic goals it set when first making the investment.

Perspective: Top Three Things Essential to Intel Capital's Relevance and Longevity

1. **Ability to sense where Intel needs to go and to adapt accordingly**
   Intel Capital helps the company make sense of trends and uses investments to gain insights the corporation can translate into learning (e.g., landscape of start-ups/tech and flag gaps). As the "eyes and ears" of Intel and by delivering returns greater than Intel's weighted average cost of capital, Intel Capital essentially is "paid to learn" about what is happening in the technology ecosystem.

2. **CVC/VC Ecosystem Collaboration and Leadership Position**
   Intel Capital maintains an active role in CVC/VC investment ecosystem to not only guarantee continued access to the best deals with complementary, like-minded partners but also to deliver incremental value to the entrepreneurs it serves. With the growing power and influence of savvy CVCs in key sectors, Intel is pioneering innovation partnering programs and syndicates of investors that bring "more than money"—who look to collaborate in complementary pursuits of new techs and market segments. By working together with those who share this vision of bringing significant corporate leverage and sophisticated business guidance, the VC community can accelerate the progress of their collective portfolio companies.

3. **Commitment to CV program practice excellence**
   Intel Capital has survived and thrived over the years by constantly assessing the needs of their portfolio companies, the needs of their corporate parent, the competitive landscape, the financial and economic environment, and Intel Capital's capabilities and gaps. Intel Capital regularly adapts and refines both investment strategy and CV program operations strategy to align and serve the interests

of all stakeholders (parent, portfolio companies, syndicate/ecosystem partners, and team members).

Intel Capital was early to establish itself as a Tier 1 VC investor and has led the way in the development of a formal and well-funded portfolio development team, with specialized CVC team design and portfolio development programs. Intel Capital also uniquely fills out its middle-level teams by "growing from within," recruiting from within Intel and formally training those candidates in Intel Capital's specialized practices, processes, and business and maintaining Intel Corporation's overall commitment to diversity and inclusion in the workforce.

Over more than twenty-five years, Intel Capital has maintained its preeminent industry leader position and has built exceptional "brand value." Even though its high-performance senior professionals are desirable recruitment targets both by VCs and other CVCs, the average tenure of Intel Capital's core managing directors remains approximately fifteen years.

How Is Intel Capital Measured?

While its investors are compensated on cash-on-cash returns, Intel Capital is judged not only on its financial returns but also its strategic relevance to Intel.

PROGRAM PROFILE: MERCK GLOBAL HEALTH INNOVATION FUND

Program Name	Merck Global Health Innovation Fund (GHI)
Date Established	2010
Parent HQ & CV Locations	Corporate Parent HQ–Kenilworth, NJ GHI Fund–HQ North America (New Jersey), Europe (Barcelona)
Charter	With a starting vision that "data will be currency" in health care, Merck GHI is chartered with building a carefully integrated portfolio of health-care solutions and services complementary to Merck's core pharmaceuticals and vaccines businesses. As a strategic growth investor, GHI's goal is to grow emerging health-care solutions into meaningful businesses.
Legal Structure	• LLC (Evergreen fund) • Reports to head of Corporate Strategy and Financial Planning
CV Program Elements	• Minority equity investing (CVC) • Majority equity investing–"roll-ups" / M&A opportunities (growth equity) • Portfolio success management (CV and partner business development / consulting, facilitating portfolio strategic landing spots)
Team Size (8)	• President, GHI Fund (externally recruited) • CVC–7 (primarily external recruits): 5 MDs, 1 principal, 1 analyst • Portfolio success management (strategic outsource while in development)
Focus Areas	<u>Goal:</u> Combine emerging informational tools with existing health data while leveraging Health IT platforms to enable innovative solutions that can improve the quality of health outcomes achieved and lower overall health system costs.

	<u>Key investment sectors</u>: Therapy planning, care management, e-clinical trials, and health analytics/artificial intelligence–all in therapeutic areas aligned with Merck's core businesses, particularly oncology.
Program Scale	• $500 million fund (evergreen) • 40+ digital health investments, 10 exits • Typically, about 25 active portfolio companies • Annually, the fund typically does 4-6 new deals • Typical minority investment size is $5-10 million, but GHI will invest significantly more as appropriate to the opportunity, e.g., roll-ups and M&A • Through the Merck Health Innovation PE Fund, GHI has access to an additional pool of money for larger growth equity deals of $50-100 million+
Recent Sample Investments	• TriNetX • Syapse • Navigating Cancer • Prognos • Livongo
Select Syndicate Partners	• VC/PE: 7Wire, Ascension, Baird Capital, Deerfield, Excel, Flare, Harbert, Heritage, HLM, General Catalyst • CVC: GE Ventures, Safeguard Scientifics, Zaffre, UPMC, Humana, United Health Group, Boston Scientific, Samsung, Johnson & Johnson, Cigna, Pfizer

Description of Program Development Journey and Key Learnings

Merck, a 101-year-old pharmaceutical company, set out to create a CVC program in 2010 and recruited J&J corporate venturing veteran Bill Taranto to lead it. GHI quickly implemented

- a vision for an emerging digital health market, with "data as currency" at its heart and for its trajectory in reshaping the business of health care;
- an adaptable, strategy-driven framework designed to create options for Merck to extend into adjacent digital health innovation areas complementary to its core pharma businesses;
- an accelerated eighteen-month program development plan for Merck Global Health Innovation (GHI).

A combination of factors allowed GHI to meet development milestones twice as fast as many other CV programs:

- The emerging digital health adjacency investment focus limited the need for the overwhelming parent educational/operational engagement that many programs face
- A specialized CV program legal structure, funding strategy, and governance model was designed to ensure "freedom to operate" in pursuit of a charter outside of the core Merck pharma regulatory context
- A lean, experienced team (internal/external blend) was supported by strategic outsourcing for specialized CV and labor-intensive functions

The team started by systematically mapping and landscaping opportunities to drive the development of GHI's unique ecosystem approach to digital health investing and partnering, framing the interrelationships and categorization of prospective venture and partner targets, and creating a foundational platform for creating multipliers of value in the GHI portfolio. Early on, the team recognized the power of strategic communications and excelled at communicating the power of the GHI health-care ecosystem vision and set of investment theses to Merck executives, potential partners, and portfolio companies.

However, being early to the digital health investing party, GHI has had to continuously balance the timing of opportunity maturation: accelerating the development of emerging digital health subsectors and laying the foundation for the parent Merck, when ready, to engage with the technology and business opportunities GHI serves up in alignment with priority therapy areas.

In the succeeding years, marked by massive changes in health care and several leadership changes within Merck, GHI's starting vision of digital health ("data as currency") and its ecosystem approach to its portfolio and partnering strategy have remained remarkably consistent and timely. GHI has further increased the horsepower of its digital health imprint and optionality with geographic expansion of the team and the extension of its investment tool kit to drive market acceleration through direct growth equity investing and partnerships (e.g., portfolio rollups, M&A).

The result: in eight years, GHI has turned its $500 million fund evergreen, has invested in over forty digital health investments, and has realized ten exits (25 percent), and over half of their portfolio companies have developed meaningful commercial relationships with Merck—all solid indicators that GHI has created a high-performance "impact delivery engine" that operates predictably at scale.

Key Program Design Elements:

- **Strategy-driven investment framework**

    GHI Fund uses an outside-in view to develop its investment theses independent of Merck's business lines, defining potential strategic options for the business. GHI has operational freedom to pursue deals that have option value—the potential to create future value that may not yet be on the radar of the current business.

- **Ecosystem thinking**

    There are few point solutions that are successful in health care, so GHI Fund deploys an "ecosystem" approach. This starts with defining a critical problem in the market, identifying the solution components that would need to be integrated, then developing an "ecosystem view"—which categorically maps where elements of the "solution stack" may be sourced and how they interrelate, from technologies to shared platforms and apps, to delivery mechanisms and value chains. This integrated ecosystem view essentially becomes a unique strategic frame for identifying high-value investment and partner opportunities for GHI, aligning with GHI's investment themes, defining potential paths to parent company impact, and accelerating and, in some cases, multiplying the points of value creation by guiding/arranging for collaboration among GHI's portfolio companies and partners.

- **Team design—Strategic outsourcing to augment lean core team**

  The initial GHI core team of high-performing professionals has remained intact and continues to be lean by design. Taranto has, from the start, championed strategic partnering and outsourcing as a strategy for augmenting core team capabilities and GHI operations with experienced specialty professionals, as a means for adding high-quality functions without increasing headcount, piloting new initiatives before operationalizing them, expanding geographic or technology related depth without ownership, etc. This lean core/strategic outsourcing approach has been a factor in the continuing agility and adaptability of GHI's business models, personnel development and career planning.

- **Collaboration and accountability with Merck business lines**

  While GHI has maintained operational freedom, it has forged close strategic ties to Merck's core businesses and the Merck execs who are driving them. GHI's investment board is comprised of senior business leaders who also have the responsibility to and accountability for championing portfolio companies within the business lines. Through an expedited process, there are additional budget dollars available for impact investing that combines commercial deals with equity deals. This allows GHI to operate at venture speed, not corporate speed.

Best Example of How Business Model Works: Preventice

Early in its existence GHI identified atrial fibrillation as an area that would benefit greatly from deploying passive monitoring technology. GHI invested in a Mayo Clinic spin-out named Preventice that had the ability to passively monitor and predict atrial fibrillation and then issue real-time alerts to the patient and caregivers.

Preventice's solution provided an extensible monitoring platform but lacked the back-end care management and fulfillment capabilities. GHI funded acquisitions of two other companies to provide these solutions, enabling Preventice to offer a market-leading end-to-end solution.

Providing an integrated offering has positioned Preventice as a market leader in cardiovascular monitoring and has it positioned for IPO.

Perspective: Top Three Things Deemed Essential to Merck GHI's Program Development and Scale

- **Freedom to operate as a VC fund**

    Operating as part of a pharma company in a regulated industry: As with all CVC programs, GHI must work hard to remain relevant to its parent corporation and business units. Making this particularly challenging is the nature of a life sciences industry that is undergoing significant change through digital disruption but is still subject to significant regulatory and legal constraints.

- **Access to committed capital**

    With an expansive ecosystem view of digital health opportunities, GHI will continue to explore access to diverse sources and types of venture and innovation funding to complement the existing CVC evergreen fund and GHI innovation PE Fund.

- **Need to hire/retain specialist team**

    GHI's lean operating model underlines the importance of retaining/expanding the core investment team as well as the ability to recruit and tap both in-house and outsourced portfolio development ("portfolio success management") resources. This is particularly important as the level of commercial engagement with the

Merck parent increases. The team has an ongoing dialogue with parent HR to develop competitive but Merck-appropriate compensation and career path approaches.

Note: As with all CVC programs at point of expansion and scale, maintaining an intentionally lean core team of senior CVC professionals while rapidly expanding its numbers of portfolio companies has the potential to create a bandwidth problem in terms of the number of board seats being handled per person and introducing more risk/corporate exposure.

How Is Merck GHI Measured?

GHI is measured by standard financial metrics, as well as softer strategic ones:

- Financial metrics:
  o Return on investment
  o IRR
  o Cash returned toward evergreen status
- Strategic metrics:
  o Market insights and external recognition of thought leadership
  o Impacts of commercial relationships with Merck business units
  o Access to novel technologies, capabilities, and data
  o Talent and culture impact
  o Option value (to expand into new business lines)

WHAT'S NEXT...

The Evolution of Corporate Venturing

Once upon a time, venture capital was a niche industry helping entrepreneurs grow by providing capital and advice, and corporations mainly tried to be like VCs.

Every day, corporations would look at deals brought to them by VCs and would be asked to pay a premium to join the round or buy the portfolio company.

One day, after the global financial crisis and as the implications of Henry Chesbrough's open innovation theory, published in 2003, became better understood, corporations decided venturing was more strategic to their future.

Because of that they set up CVCs as part of their innovation tool set and invested more time, support, and money to find deals, lead them, and help portfolio companies impact their parents.

Consequently, the venture industry and CVCs started to change. They became larger and global and more strategic, and began to show financial gains, and developed their own professional requirements.

Until finally venture was recognized as a service-orientated profession helping entrepreneurs with their five primary needs of capital, customers, product development, hiring, and an exit, and corporations opened up their value creation and shareholder returns options via three primary phases of CV program evolution:

Phase 1: Years 0–3 (Start-up)	Phase 2: Years 4–6 (Expansion)	Phase 3: Years 7–9+ (Resiliency)

The Next Generation

Evolution, however, has yet to rest. What can be done, will be. To paraphrase Wendell Brooks in his foreword: business and societies change; we are yet to reach the end of history.

A focus on risk and return in broadly open economies has driven unprecedented wealth creation. But the next few decades seem likely to be ones driven by a wider geopolitical context.

Understanding the impact of the work being done in business and how the combinations of entrepreneurs and innovation capital can affect all stakeholders could increasingly decide your success and how we together can make the world a better place.

AFTERWORD

I fundamentally believe Corporate Venturing is an innovation discipline that is here to stay—in service to its corporate parents as well as the external entrepreneurial ecosystem, shaping a path from the present to the future.

CV is uniquely placed to detect signals from noise, define investable growth themes and bring the "outside-in" and the "inside-out." Resourceful CV teams create opportunities for impactful collaborations among the corporate parent, customers, entrepreneurs and other investment and market development partners.

If there's one constant in business — it's change. The digitization of everything is disrupting the world as we know it and no industry or corporation is immune. To compete in this fourth industrial revolution, companies must reimagine their business models with customer experience at the core and envision new ways for customers to access product solutions.

In a world where the pace of change will never be as slow as it is today, corporations can no longer go it alone. CV has become a crucial strategic complement to traditional R&D and an increasingly mainstream innovation discipline for the Fortune 500.

Focusing on adjacent and transformational as well as core spaces, specialist CV teams help businesses and corporate strategists see around corners, identify emerging innovation signals in the entrepreneurial ecosystem, and translate them into growth opportunities. And it's not just about science and technology—in these times, it has become very clear that business model innovation is just as necessary as technological breakthroughs.

At GE Ventures, we put these principles to work in pioneering a "nextgen" multi-modal innovation model. Over the past five years, the program has evolved to incorporate venture capital investing (CVC), licensing, business creation and new market development modalities—all with an eye toward building companies to create value, drive growth, transform industries, solve customer challenges and impact lives. During this time, we invested in 100+ companies with strong returns, incubated 9 new companies which provided future growth optionality and created value for GE businesses and shareholders. We commercialized GE's IP and developed new markets by working in partnership with key thought leaders and entrepreneurial scientists. Most importantly, this multi-modal innovation model has provided multiple growth pathways for our businesses, helped to increase productivity and effectiveness, and enabled entry into new markets. GE's businesses have enthusiastically adopted the entrepreneurial ecosystem and non-traditional partnerships into their business strategies.

The strategic ability to determine when—and how—to build, buy or partner is fundamental to corporate growth and value capture through engagement with entrepreneurs. It is within today's challenging and opportunity-rich environment that corporate venturing programs have become the vital "tip of the spear," bridging the entrepreneurial ecosystem and global corporations to create innovation optionality.

I have been privileged to hold corporate, entrepreneurial and venture capital positions over my 35+ year career. I have seen all three sectors evolve and increasingly work together around a shared goal: turning untapped potential into real value. Over the past five years, I have seen big leaps forward in the evolution of the corporate venturing practice—sophisticated and well-funded CV programs staffed with high performance investment and business development professionals. All of these elements have come together to fast-track program performance and boost global recognition of corporate venturing's essential value.

Looking ahead, I foresee CV programs and professionals continuing to provide both financial and strategic value to parent companies, as part of an enduring quest to transform possibility into viability and deliver the next big thing. All of us feel the market pressure to innovate faster and better, and corporate venturing is an essential vehicle in that race. With the assistance of Corporate Venturing: A Survival Guide, our community now has the story of the evolution of Corporate Venturing as a mainstream corporate discipline, a vision of what sets the next generation of high performer CV programs and teams apart, and a map to creative options and pathways for more agile, accelerated development and continuous impact.

Sue Siegel
Chief Innovation Officer, GE and CEO, GE Ventures

About the Authors

Heidi Mason / Managing Partner, Bell Mason Group has spent more than twenty-five years in Silicon Valley, immersed in its ecosystem and venture-backed start-up community, as an entrepreneur focusing on start-up development and corporate venturing (CV) consulting. She cofounded the Bell Mason Group in 1990, a specialty management consultancy dedicated to improving corporate venture program development and impact. Mason developed the corporate venturing framework and assessment methodology that serves as a foundation for much of the Bell Mason Group work. BMG clients have spanned the globe, across industry sectors, including Citigroup, Merck, Chevron, Philips, and Coca Cola. She has held numerous venture board seats over the years, along with strategic advisory board roles with large, global companies. Under her leadership, BMG has partnered with a variety of leading CV specialty service providers to accelerate quality CV program and platform development (in legal, compensation, innovation strategy, and accounting/tax). She has also been instrumental in guiding industry research and standards development that support CV practice professionalization and quality repeatability. She became a Strategic Advisory Board member for Global Corporate Venturing shortly after its founding in 2010. She is also a multipublished author (including *The Venture Imperative: A New Model of Corporate Innovation*, Harvard Business School Press).

Mason holds a degree from the University of Pennsylvania, where she graduated with honors.

Liz Arrington / Partner, Bell Mason Group has spent decades advising global corporations on the development of best-practice venturing and innovation programs, with emphasis on performance management strategies and systems. She also collaborates with leading industry organizations such as Health Evolution Summit, J Thelander, and Global Corporate Venturing to develop specialist

CV content and professional programs. She has worked extensively with venture-capital-backed start-ups around the globe to address nascent market development opportunities. Arrington began her corporate venturing career with Mitsubishi International Corporation, in Silicon Valley, where she and Mason were first introduced. She subsequently spent eight years in Asia, where she cofounded the Asia-Pacific practice of VIA international, a global "routes to market" consultancy, and pioneered the firm's venturing advisory practice. Shortly thereafter, she joined forces with BMG and spearheaded its successful introduction into ASEAN, North Asia, Australia, and New Zealand. Arrington relocated to Silicon Valley in 2001.

Arrington is a director of Tack Gives Back, a nonprofit supporting equine- and other animal-facilitated therapy organizations. She holds an MBA in marketing and finance from the Wharton School of the University of Pennsylvania, and an honors undergraduate degree from Harvard College.

James Mawson / CEO, Global Corporate Venturing, has twenty years of financial and technology journalism, including roles at Financial Times Business, Dow Jones, Wall Street Journal and Thomson Reuters. As well as editing Private Equity News, James coordinated leveraged buyout and venture capital coverage for use by other titles in the Dow Jones and News Corporation group and acted as a spokesman on BBC radio and television. In 2010 Mawson founded Mawsonia, the publishing company he leads as CEO and editor-in-chief, and from which he launched Global Corporate Venturing (GCV); this was followed by the launch of his second publication, Global University Venturing (GUV) in 2012 and the third, Global Government Venturing (GGV), in 2014. Mawson is a widely acknowledged speaker, a published author, and a pioneering force behind development of the preeminent media and events company providing the community with forums for exchange, data and information resources, and collaboration and workflow tools, such as GCV Connect and GCV Analytics, under the GCV Leadership Society, the new and improved professional trade organization that serves global corporate venturing and innovation (CV&I) professionals. The GCV Academy also offers professional development curricula and training courses for aspiring professionals and other corporate personnel who need to improve their skills and better understand corporate venturing practices and program structures.

He is also a director of the London Press Club and has acted as a pro bono editor for the European Venture Philanthropy Association monthly newsletter. Mawson graduated from King's College, London.

BMG/GCV Collaboration

BMG & GCV initiated the CV Trends & Insights Project in 2017, as an effort to document five years of rapid and remarkable change in corporate venturing strategies, program design, and development. The inaugural report capped a look at the last five years' explosive growth of global corporate venturing programs, highlighting the professionalization of CVC specialty practices and the standardization of foundational CVC team roles and market rate compensation bands, and noting the progressive acknowledgment of CVC as a "mainstream" contributor to corporate innovation strategy and growth.

In 2018, research zeroed in on end-to-end investing, fast becoming the unique hallmark of corporate venturing. The reports highlighted the latest trends in dedicated CVC and CVBD teams, expanded tool sets, and innovatively integrated programs, with growing clarity around strategic and financial measures and metrics. It is this collaboration and its output that served as the starting point for *Corporate Venturing: A Survival Guide.*

INDEX